# HOW TO HEAL USING INTUITIVE HEALING

A journey to a whole you

*By*
**Dr Irina Webster**

A catalogue record for this book is available from the National Library of Australia

Copyright © 2021 Dr Irina Webster

All rights reserved. No part of this publication may be reproduced, stored in a retrieval system, or transmitted in any form or by any means, electronic, mechanical, photocopying, recording or otherwise without prior permission of the author.

**Publisher:**
Inspiring Publishers
P.O. Box 159, Calwell, ACT Australia 2905
Email: publishaspg@gmail.com
http://www.inspiringpublishers.com

National Library of Australia Cataloguing-in-Publication entry

Author: Webster, Dr Irina

Title: **How to Heal Using Intuitive Healing: A journey to a whole you**/*Dr Irina Webster*

ISBN: 978-0-6451228-3-1 (pbk)
      978-0-6451228-4-8 (ebook)

I live by the motto that
*healing* is *always* possible.

Even if the problems are big and illnesses are severe – believe in healing …

Our body is designed to heal,
and your job is to facilitate healing.

# TABLE OF CONTENT

*Introduction to Intuitive Healing and Medical Intuition* ............... 10

*Why people dismiss intuitions* ............................................................ 13

**Chapter 1: Intuitive Mind vs Logic Mind** ........................................ 15

The Structure of the Intuitive (non-linear) Mind .......................... 17

How Intuitive Healing Can Help with Body Control .................... 19

Scientific Evidence for Intuitive Healing ........................................ 21

**Chapter 2: How I Got into This Intuition Business** ...................... 28

**Chapter 3: Our Energy Anatomy** ...................................................... 36

**Chapter 4: Our Energy Centres (CHAKRAS)** ................................. 40

The 1st Chakra: The Power of Family and Tribe ........................... 41

The 2nd Chakra: The Power of Relationships and Creativity ...... 50

The 3rd Chakra: The Personal Power and Self-Esteem ................ 57

The 4th Chakra: The Power of Unconditional Love ...................... 64

The 5th Chakra: The Power of Communication and Faith .......... 72

The 6th Chakra: The Power of the Mind and the
  Higher-Self Intuition ................................................................. 79

The 7th Chakra: Our Divine Connection and Life Purpose ......... 84

**Chapter 5: The Spiritual Design** ............................................. 91

Chakra Scan Meditation ............................................................ 92

Reading Energy on Other People ............................................. 98

**Chapter 6: Chakras Questions** ............................................... 99

**Chapter 7: How to Heal Chakras** ........................................... 113

**Chapter 8: How to Remove the Energy of Illness from your Organs** ............................................. 117

**Chapter 9: Working with the Aura** ....................................... 125

How to Scan Your Own Aura .................................................... 128

How to Scan the Aura on Another Person ............................ 129

How to Clean the Aura .............................................................. 132

How to Re-Create the Aura ...................................................... 134

**Chapter 10: Body Shapes** ....................................................... 139

**Chapter 11: How to Differentiate Intuition from Fear, Brain Chatter and Other False Perceptions** .......... 141

**Chapter 12: How to Stop Fear – the Internal Smile** ........ 147

Chakras and the Effect of the Internal Smile ....................... 149

**Chapter 13: Intuitive Healing for Relationships** ................ 151

How to differentiate Intuition from Fear in Relationships ......... 155

Chakras and Relationships ....................................................... 157

**Chapter 14: Intuitive Healing for Parents** ........................... 159

Chakras and Inner Child Healing ............................................. 165

**Chapter 15: Intuitive Healing Through Dreams,
Visions and Hypnagogic States** ...................167

Types of Dreams ...........................................................171

How to Work with Dreams ........................................174

**Chapter 16: Intuitive Eating - Healing with Food** ..........178

How to Clean and Energise Your Food ....................181

Energetic Meaning of Food .......................................183

How Food Influences Chakras ................................. 186

**Chapter 17: How to Forgive** .............................................191

How Does Forgiveness Affect Chakras? ..................194

**Chapter 18: Charting Your Progress** ............................. 196

Intuitive Healing Tables ............................................. 199

    Table 1: Organ Meanings ...................................... 199

    Table 2: Symptoms and Illnesses Meanings .............. 207

*Afterword* ..........................................................................241

*About the Author* ........................................................... 244

*Bibliography* ....................................................................245

*Also Available from Dr Irina Webster* ........................ 248

# New Scientific Evidence ...

*My dear friend*

*Have you found yourself resonating with the new scientific evidence released by neuroscience recently, which has proven that under the right conditions, the body has the power to heal itself from even the most, 'incurable,' illnesses?*

*The key words here are – 'under the right conditions' ... What are these conditions and how do we create them? This is what you will discover in this book.*

# Introduction to Intuitive Healing and Medical Intuition

Let me introduce Intuitive Healing and Medical Intuition to you. Everything that I regard as having high value in life comes from this topic. I feel truly honoured to be involved with this amazing subject, which has transformed my life and helped me become an empowered and whole person.

Intuitive healing is the art of connecting to our body using our own intuition. Intuition is the natural ability to understand something instinctively without the need for conscious reasoning. We are all born with intuitive abilities, and this is not a special talent but rather a skill that we can develop.

When you start listening to your intuition, you realise that we do not really need the help of outsiders for as much information as we think; if we would only trust our own instincts. Our intuition is the inner physician that we all have.

Look at your life experiences and you will find that you have already experienced intuition many times, (but maybe did not pay enough attention to value it).

1. When you are around some people do you feel drained?
2. Have you ever felt that someone was staring at you?
3. Have you ever felt instant liking or disliking for someone?

4. *Have you ever been able to sense how someone is feeling, despite how this person was acting?*
5. *Have you ever been able to sense another person's presence before you actually heard or saw the person?*
6. *Do certain sounds, colours and fragrances make you feel more comfortable or uncomfortable?*
7. *Do some rooms make you want to stay? Or leave?*
8. *Have you ever ignored or shoved aside a first impression of someone, only to find that it bears itself out eventually?*

If you answered 'Yes' to any of these questions – you have experienced **survival intuitions** that warned you about other people or situations.

**This survival sense is also attuned to our health.** Medical intuition is our intuitive ability to understand our own health and wellbeing. If we listen to our medical intuition – we can prevent illnesses and heal them much faster. Although we may not all be attuned to our medical intuition, we are all born with this ability to feel and understand our bodies.

This book will help you become attuned to your own **medical intuitive voice**.

## Case study of how sensing the subtle energy inside the body stopped dangerous health problems ...

*Diseases never appear just out of the blue. Subtle changes precede most physical symptoms. If you catch imbalances in your body before you have pain or a full-blown disease you can stop the problem before it begins.*

*Listen to Anna's story ...*

*Anna suffered gallstone attacks a few times a year. She often ended up in hospital on morphine. Her doctor recommended surgery but she did not want that. I taught Anna how to do body scans on herself, (body scan is the ability to sense and observe your own subtle body energy).*

*As a result of this observation, she noticed something quite interesting. She noticed that for a day or two before an attack her abdominal area would feel bloated and warm, these special sensations only came just before an attack. She used this newfound knowledge and the next time she felt the same feelings, she took medicine. From that day her gallbladder attacks became less and less severe and finally she managed to stop them for good. This skilful observation of her own subtle energy fluctuations in her body broke the pain cycle before the actual symptoms occurred.*

# Why People Dismiss Intuitions

If intuition is our natural voice, why do people ignore intuitions?

- The voice of intuition is a very subtle and gentle voice. It often comes in a flash and is difficult to anchor physically unless you are very aware.
- The sound of brain chatter is loud, continuous, and overpowering. It is not possible to hear intuition if you are listening to brain chatter.
- The voices of fear are even louder than brain chatter. If someone is in fear mode, it is not possible for them to hear intuition, especially medical intuition. Many people are in fear mode, most of the time.
- From a young age we are programmed to use our 'logic mind,' for example being told as a child to, "Just think with your head." Nobody taught you how to feel and sense.
- We often dismiss intuitions because we do not like the information we are receiving. Intuition can ask you to leave a relationship or a job, but because of the sense of loyalty or survival fears, you stay.

We sense intuitions with the non-linear mind which I call the Intuitive mind. You cannot sense intuitions with the Logic mind. You can try it, because it is always good to try everything - but it will not work. To understand the intuitive process, let me explain the structure of our mind first.

# Chapter 1:
# INTUITIVE MIND VS LOGIC MIND

Our mind has two parts: The Logic mind and the Intuitive mind. People also call it conscious and subconscious.
We sense intuitions and energy with our Intuitive mind (also called non-linear mind). The Logic mind does not deal with intuition. It does not matter how much you think about intuition, you cannot sense it unless you switch off your Logic mind and switch on your Intuitive mind.

## How Big is the Intuitive Mind?

According to neuroscience, if you take the whole mind as 100%, then the Logic mind takes no more than 5-10% of the whole mind capacity. The Intuitive part takes 90-95% of the whole mind capacity. Therefore, the Intuitive mind is the biggest part of our consciousness but the least understood.

Here are some **sad statistics**:

> Most people live their life and die using no more than 10% of their mind capacity. They use only their Logic mind - rational, thinking, calculating, dealing with physical matters part.
>
> They have never been taught how to use their Intuitive mind - the part of consciousness that works with feelings and sensations. These people often deny, dismiss, and do not trust their feelings.

## The Intuitive Mind Structure

Let us look at some Intuitive mind facts:

- The Intuitive mind takes 90-95% of the whole consciousness, therefore it is the biggest part.
- It is your responsibility to develop this part of the mind because conventional systems do not teach us how to feel and sense. They teach us how to use the smallest part of consciousness - the Logic mind, which is also important but insufficient if used alone, without the Intuitive mind.
- The Intuitive mind has two parts: The Subconscious mind and the Unconscious mind. Many people think they are the same, but they are not the same. They both are parts of the Intuitive mind, but they are responsible for different functions.

# The Structure of the Intuitive (Non-Linear) Mind

## It has two parts – the Subconscious and the Unconscious:

➤ The Subconscious mind refers to our feelings, emotions and sensations. Our automatic behaviours and deep beliefs are also located in the subconscious mind. That is why when we try to work on a health problem or a relationship problem using only our Logic mind, we fail.

Logic 10%

Subconscious 50-60%

Unconscious 30-40%

➤ The Unconscious mind refers to the unconscious processes in our body such as digestion, respiration, perspiration, body temperature, waterworks, pulse, heartbeat, tissue growth, regeneration, blood pressure, metabolism, hormone production, etc.

The Unconscious mind regulates organ functions: the ailments which send us to the doctors for medical attention.

The question arises –

What if we had more control over our Unconscious mind?

**Answer:** We would not need medical help as often as we do. We can just tune into our organs and correct their function. I am not suggesting you ignore medical help, not at all, I am asking you to accept the fact that we have much more control over our bodies and organs then we realise.

## HOW TO HEAL USING INTUITIVE HEALING

## Here is the Physical Proof:

> Take, for example, yogis, people who live in the East and practice yoga. They can go into meditation and slow their breathing rate and heartbeat down to zero. You look at the person and think that he is dead. But after a time, they revive themselves and restore their vital functions back to normal. This is the degree of body control they have achieved.

> Another example is a diver who is trained to go deep sea diving and survive the extreme atmospheric pressures and cold temperatures that would kill a non-trained human. He has achieved a body regulation that allows him to maintain his core temperature in extreme conditions and has trained his organs to resist the severe atmospheric pressure and not to collapse when in deep water.

> Here is the most interesting example: A famous historic figure Grigori Rasputin – a Russian monk who grew up in a village surrounded by Siberian cedars has been a subject of fascination for his superhuman ability to survive. His body was absolutely resistant to poisons, beatings, and even shootings. There are no medical explanations for his survival abilities, but there are many descriptions of how powerful he was, and how he could control his own body in extreme situations and environments in which any other human would die.

I believe that with practice, everybody can control their own body and organs at least at some level. People just need to understand the power of their Intuitive mind and practice connecting to it.

## How Intuitive Healing Can Help with Body Control

I have already explained that our Intuitive mind has two parts: the Subconscious and the Unconscious.

The Subconscious mind deals with our feelings, emotions, sensations, deep beliefs, and automatic behaviours.

The Unconscious mind deals with organ control – the functioning of our organs. It deals with digestion, respirations, metabolism, hormone productions, temperature regulation, regeneration, circulation etc …

> **Intuitive Healing helps to connect to both parts of the Intuitive Mind: the Subconscious mind and the Unconscious mind.**

When you are working with **emotions**: understanding emotions, excavating trapped emotions, changing emotions, using positive affirmations – you are working with the **Subconscious mind**.

When you are working with **energy**: sensing subtle body energy, feeling the energy in the organs, correcting the energy flow in the organs - you are working with the **Unconscious mind**.

On the table below you see how to differentiate when you are dealing with the Subconscious mind and when you are dealing with the Unconscious mind.

# HOW TO HEAL USING INTUITIVE HEALING

| The Subconscious mind (working with emotions) | The Unconscious mind. (working with energy) |
|---|---|
| Feeling emotions | Sensing subtle energy in the body and organs |
| Working with Affirmations | Doing the energetic body scan, scanning the body and organs energetically |
| Changing emotional patterns from negative to positive | Removing the toxic energy from the organs using energy healing techniques |
| Empowering yourself using self-talk. | Strengthening organs energetically using energy healing techniques. |

To heal your life, you need to work with both - the Subconscious and the Unconscious mind. Working only with one part is insufficient and can be a reason why some people do not heal.

Some healing modalities, like reiki, for example, only focus on working with energy but do not look at the emotional components of the problem. It means they only address the Unconscious mind but do not address the Subconscious mind during the healing process. This approach may not be enough to heal properly.

Some healing modalities only work with emotional problems – psychotherapy or counselling, for example. Again, this approach is not enough to heal properly because they only deal with the Subconscious mind, (emotions and feelings), but do not deal with the Unconscious mind, (the energy inside the body).

## Scientific Evidence for Intuitive Healing

Recently, we had a great deal of scientific evidence released by neuroscience, stating that under the right conditions, the body has the power to heal itself from even the most, 'incurable,' illnesses.

More importantly that we can facilitate natural healing by understanding the energy of the process, especially the energy of our emotions – the hidden causes of most illnesses, symptoms, pains, aches, and conditions.

I am not saying that the other factors do not contribute to developing health problems. Of course, our environment, genetics and food play a big role in our health, but behind every illness, pain and ache, there is an emotional component. Many emotions are hidden inside our cells. They create cellular memories. Cellular memories are trapped emotions which often originate from the time of birth and beyond. Some trapped emotions come from our past lives, such as collective traumas. Collective traumas stay inside the cells of a whole family, a group, a culture or even a generation.

> For example, I noticed that many Russians of my age have cellular memories of wars. Although they were born in the 70s – a long time after the Second World War finished, their psyche is affected by the war experiences. These cellular memories negatively affect their health and their relationships.
>
> Many times, when talking to Russian women of my age, I saw an image of 'a grieving widow.' On a physical level, they had

> living husbands, but their relationship problems were connected to grief, loss, sadness, guilt, and shame, as if they were widows, but they were not. Their health problems reflect their emotions in most cases.
>
> When talking to Russian men of my age, I often noticed an image of, 'a wounded soldier,' who witnessed killing, and himself also participating in killing - totally unintentionally, just because of the war. On a physical level, they did not experience a war, but their emotional problems were connected to the traumas as if they were 'wounded warriors.'
>
> **I call it a 'cultural trauma' or a 'generational trauma.'**

> Some Australians have cellular memories of convicts, these memories stop them from moving forward in life.
>
> Many times, when working with people, I saw an image of a chain around their feet – a symbol of imprisonment that came from the past lives of convicts. On all occasions, these people had problems with moving forward, starting fresh and forgiving. Another great example of a 'cultural trauma.'

Only with the help of Intuitive healing it is possible to excavate these trapped emotions and release them.

Until these trapped emotions are understood and released, the illness stays in the body.

Now, if you are still sceptical, I would like to show you more physical proof that healing is always possible.

## Spontaneous Remission Project

You can look no further than the Spontaneous Remission Project: a database from the Institute of Noetic Sciences with over 3,500 case studies in their medical literature, of patients who recovered from seemingly, 'incurable' illnesses without medical treatment, or treatment that is considered inadequate to produce the disappearance of the disease, symptoms or tumours.

I personally looked at this database and found everything was there: stage 4 cancers, autoimmune illnesses, severe depressions, neurological disorders, and other disabilities. Spontaneous remissions were documented in almost every so called, 'incurable' illness. They also described what people did and what the most common traits were of people who recovered from the, 'incurable' illness. The conclusion was that there is no such thing as an 'incurable' illness, but the body must create the right conditions to heal. This is the clue.

## 'The Placebo Effect'

The other interesting fact, 'the placebo effect' is a thorn in the side of the medical establishment, because the effectiveness of all drugs is tested against the 'placebo drugs' before medicines are released for public use.

Placebo results ...

We've known this since the 1950s, that if you give people a fake treatment—a sugar pill, a saline injection, or most effectively, fake surgery, 18-80% of the time people get better, and it's not just in their mind but in their body and this is measurable.

For example, patients getting placebos were found to have ulcers that healed, colons that became less inflamed, bronchi that dilated, warts that disappeared, biopsy cells looking different under the microscope.

So, who and what was the healer in all these placebo cases? Obviously, it was not the doctors and not the treatment ... You can say that the body healed itself, but it is only partially true, because if the person did not go to hospital and did not receive the fake treatment, they would still be sick.

The answer I found is that faith or deep unconditional beliefs in the treatment creates the changes in the body that make people heal.

## What Can You Do?

You do not need to wait until you go to doctors and get a placebo treatment. You cannot ask for it. If you know that you are getting a placebo, it will not be effective.

But the truth is, **you are your own placebo**. You create placebos every moment of your life. Every thought and every feeling you have are your placebos: negative or positive.

There are negative placebos called, 'nocebo' which are negative expectations, doubt, cynicism, lack of trust. This kind of placebo, 'nocebo,' creates illnesses and problems.

There are positive placebos, which are faith, trust, surrendering, love, living in the present moment and having a positive outlook on life. These placebos create healing.

So, the truth is that the body can heal itself using this natural healing intelligence and we can help, guide, and regulate this process with the power of our thoughts and emotions. This is what Intuitive Healing is all about.

# Faith and Healing

From my experience with healing (myself and others), I have come to believe that faith is the most powerful component in healing. I am not talking about religious faith but having faith in healing. It means believing that all problems can be healed, and that the universe always guides us to find balance.

## Healing and Curing

Many people are confused about these two definitions, Healing and Curing. Let me clarify ...

**Healing** is releasing underlying fears and energies, that caused the problem in the first place. Healing is always **internal,** which comes from within. Only you can do it.

**Curing** means disappearance of symptoms using external sources – pills, tablets, surgeries, procedures. It comes from the external sources and somebody else does it for you. A cure does not deal with energies, underlying emotions and fears that caused the illness in the first place. Therefore, after taking pills, tablets, surgeries or procedures, the energy of the illness is still in the body and problems come back or the illness moves from one organ to another, or complications occur.

➤ **Often, but not always,** a cure, or disappearance of symptoms follow healing. Sometimes, symptoms stay, but healing happened anyway because the fears were released.
➤ Therefore, **healing is always possible, even, if the symptoms stay**. It is always possible to release the underlying fears and energies from your body.

Nick Vujicic

For example, Nick Vujicic was born without limbs. Despite his disability, he become a famous author, motivational speaker, and a successful man. He married a beautiful woman and has four healthy children. He lives an independent life, and he is a true example of healing. He is not sick. He managed to release all the fears associated with his condition, but the symptoms stay - he still does not have limbs. He is a real proof that the power of human spirit is stronger than physical limitations. This is what healing is all about.

> **The power of the human spirit is stronger than physical limitations.**
>
> **This is what healing is all about.**
>
> **Therefore, healing is always possible even if the symptoms stay.**

## Healing Comes from Understanding Your Own Body.

The concept of healing is not new; the Ancient Greeks knew about it.

- ➤ **Know Thyself** - The Ancient Greek aphorism, inscribed on the Temple of Apollo at Delphi.
- ➤ Healing comes from understanding your vulnerabilities and fears and not denying them.
- ➤ Healing comes from understanding your own Energy Anatomy, because fears are negative energies that we keep in our emotional centres called chakras.

*'Know Thyself' inscription on the Temple of Apollo at Delphi.*

## Why Healing is Possible

Why is healing possible? Why can the most dangerous illnesses be healed?

Here is the scientific fact: every seven years we have a new body of cells.

The human body continuously regenerates itself, from the cells in our skeleton to the nails on our toes. Some cells are replaced very quickly, some are replaced very slowly, but by the end of seven years, we have a brand-new body of cells.

The process of cell regeneration happens regardless of what we do. If you do nothing with yourself, then you will get the 'same old, same old' body in seven years' time. Most likely your problems will deteriorate because you allow the cells to replicate in a negative way. But if you guide the process of regeneration in a positive way – then you get a totally new result.

## Chapter 2:
# HOW I GOT INTO THIS INTUITION BUSINESS

Now, since I have provided all the evidence for intuitive healing and medical intuition, let me explain how I got into this business in the first place.

I have been intuitive for as long as I can remember. Even as a child, I was able to sense energy around people, although at that time I could not explain what it was. I could just feel if people were kind or not, sick, or healthy. I also felt how other people affected my body; I could experience physical pain in my body when in contact with certain people or absolute serenity and joy when with others. I had visions nobody could see. I sensed energy around people and described it in colours. "Aunt Galina always looks green like a spring leaf on a birch tree" – this is what I noticed, as a child, about my aunt who was a Pulmonologist (lung specialist) and also a great healer.

"Grandpa is so grey and brown." This is what I noticed about my grandpa who was dying from old wounds he got during the war. I could feel in colour from my childhood. My parents thought I was imagining it and did not take it seriously.

Becoming a doctor was my intuitive decision. I really wanted to learn everything about my body and help others to understand theirs.

I graduated medicine in the Northern State Medical University (Russia) in the city called Archangel (Russian pronunciation Arkhangelsk, means the city of Archangel Michael).

In my early years of being a doctor, I had a great interest in immunology and even did my post-graduation studies in this field acquiring a qualification of children Immunologist –Allergist from the Medical University of Saint-Petersburg (Russia). This seven-year practice in immunology gave me lots of insight into the human immune system and how our body gets protected from certain diseases.

In the Medical University of Saint-Petersburg, I had my first connection to a new science called Psychoneuroimmunology (Psycho means psyche, neuro is for nervous system and immunology is for immune system). This science shows the connection of the psyche (emotions) and immune response from the physical body. From there I learned that our mind has an absolute power over our body and that what we feel, and think may be even more important for our health then even our diets, exercise, or environment.

Psychoneuroimmunology research shows that negative beliefs, attitudes, emotions and generational (cultural) memories weaken our nervous and immune systems and create disease.

This concept is not new, and ancient wisdom has always encouraged us to focus on maintaining a 'healthy mind' in order to maintain a 'healthy body.' It is only now with the help of Psychoneuroimmunology that we can prove and understand this connection.

When I moved to Australia in 2001, I had to learn English first and sit many exams: English and medical. I passed the exams and then, from 2003 I worked as a doctor in the Canberra Hospital (Australia) until a certain episode in my life that transformed my life.

## My Illness was My Breakthrough

People often ask me how I become a healer ... I think it was the most natural transformation which was triggered by the necessity to heal my own wounds and learn about myself - who am I and what is my purpose in life.

My first encounter with the Intuitive Healing Power happened when I was a young woman. As a teenager and in my twenties, I suffered from a very severe eating disorder (anorexia and bulimia). I fluctuated between periods of starving myself to binging - purging for about twenty years. Conventional medicine did not help, and I was suffering silently, keeping my dark secret inside.

But once I reached rock bottom ... I was a medical student when I found myself in a lot of pain. My stomach and my back were in agony from binging-purging episodes. I did not want to take normal painkillers because they were ineffective. Without the influence of pain medications and with my pain rising, I sat on my bed holding a pillow. Then, I started to swing back and forth trying to get into the rhythm of my pain. I do not know how long I was swinging back and forth hugging the pillow before I realised that I was actually in a different state of consciousness. Soon, instead of the pain, I started to feel tingling in different parts of my body. This new sensation was pleasant and felt similar to a mild electric current. At this point, I also noticed that I was able to transfer the energy current in my body to different areas of my body simply by redirecting my attention from one part to another. What astonished me was that I could also see my organs from inside. The new energetic state I was in had opened up a new way of seeing the human body. When I moved my attention to my stomach, where I had what could accurately be called extraordinary pain, I saw a red inflamed lining with little ulcers around it. This was likely due to the continual vomiting.

Looking closer and more intently, I noticed that when my attention was on my stomach it was tingling with energy. The sensation was actually calming and pleasant. I played with this energy like a child. I do not know how long I was sitting in this state, but I eventually fell asleep. When I awoke in the morning, the pain was gone, simply gone, as if it had never existed in the first place. I felt refreshed and I felt completely different; I was transformed! My urges to binge and purge were completely gone. When I thought about binging-purging, my body quickly responded, "Oh, no – not me. I am not doing this ever again." My entire being, mind, body and spirit supported me in healing the eating disorder.

Later, I realised that this was my first experience of feeling my subtle body energy which is a vital component of intuitive healing.

The second time when energy sensing helped me heal was when I was working as a doctor at the Canberra Hospital. I suddenly developed dermatitis, or eczema which affected my hands. I had an itchy rash on my hands which progressed to multiple blisters which in turn burst. The end result made my hands look like pieces of raw meat. My colleagues prescribed a steroid cream as well as antihistamines and I was told that this condition would probably come back again and again. Being a healer in my soul, I accepted the diagnosis but not the prognosis ... I turned to healing again.

I put myself into a vibrational state – a state when you sense the vibrations of your own cells. I focused my attention on my hands and sensed the subtle body energy inside my skin, muscles, and bones. It feels like tingling and crawling sensations inside these organs.

When you can sense the subtle energy inside the organ – you can control the function of this organ. The next day, I had major improvement with the eczema. On the fifth day of healing, my hands were absolutely clean. The condition has never returned. I honestly believe that in order to heal, one must be in touch with one's own energy.

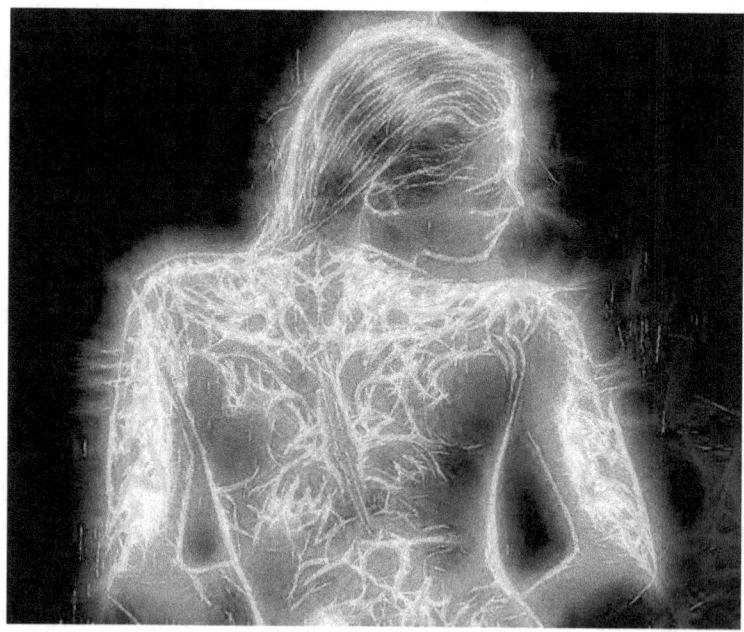

*The vibrational state.*

The final breakthrough, that made me change my occupation from totally conventional to totally unconventional was my fibroids problem. When I was working as a doctor at the Canberra Hospital, I developed a very severe uterine bleeding for which I was sent to have surgery. My gynaecologist said to me **"Irina, you will bleed to death unless you have them removed."** He was an experienced doctor in his late fifties and his words sounded like a death sentence.

At that moment, something quite extraordinary happened. I heard a small quiet voice inside me say, "Don't go. You'll be fine." It was not a loud voice; it was not a voice that made me scared or created fear. It was a very calm and subtle voice from inside my body that gave me reassurance and certainty. I did not argue with my gynaecologist. I took the operation referral and the drug script which he gave me. I went home and I had only one thought in my mind – 'I need to experience the healing state again.' So, I did. I sat down to heal myself. I went to a room where there was total peace and quiet and I was alone. I began to meditate. Once again, I felt tingling sensations in my body just as had happened during my first intuitive healing experience. Next, I moved my attention to my uterus. During my meditation, I could see a small tumour inside the lining of my uterus, I knew that it was this tumour that was causing the bleeding. Then I saw a green light inside my uterus, and this green light (like a laser) was cleaning my uterus from the inside. The experience was very calming, loving, and pleasant. The next day, my bleeding was much better. It was reduced by half or even more. I continued to perform intuitive healing two to three times a day. On the third day, the bleeding was gone completely; I have never had this problem again. Again, sensing my subtle body energy saved my health.

This experience made me become so curious about intuitive healing that I took a one-year leave from my work as a doctor and I spent the whole year studying Medical Intuition and Intuitive Healing. When this year finished, I was a different person. I felt that if I went back to conventional medicine, I would have to give people treatments that I would not take myself. Therefore, I decided to teach and help others to activate their own Intuitive Healing Power to heal their lives.

## Our Body Tells the Truth

Often, our intuitive guidance comes in a form of bodily symptoms and disease. All our pains, aches, illnesses, and conditions are messages about how we live our lives and what we need to do in order to heal.

My fibroids came with a big lesson **which taught me to see illnesses symbolically**. This illness occurred after I went through a dramatic divorce. For a long time, I suffered feelings of the 'lost love' and 'broken heart'. At times I felt that a part of my body was 'amputated'.

I needed to find meaning in my suffering, so I looked at my problems symbolically.

Uterus, where I had problems, symbolises relationships and creativity. Well, at the time, I felt that I failed to create a loving relationship.

Fibroids are tumours growing inside the uterus. Conventional medicine does not know why our bodies grow tumours, but from a spiritual point of view, tumours represent our needless and toxic thoughts and emotions that find an outlet in the organ. Again, it was clear to me that for a long time I felt 'toxic' about my relationships.

Another problem I had was severe bleeding. Symbolically, bleeding means, 'joy running out.' Here I understood a symbolic meaning of my problem and how to heal it. It was me who felt, 'toxic,' and allowed my joy to run out. I should have moved on and started creating a new life, but I was clinging to the past and created a tumour in my body.

What a great lesson I got from my illness. Our body always tells the truth about our life and what we need to do in order to heal it.

# Chapter 3:
# OUR ENERGY ANATOMY

Now, let me introduce the energy anatomy to you – the system through which the subtle energy runs.

The subtle energy enters our body at the time we are born or maybe even earlier – maybe at the time of conception. It leaves the body when we die. So, when we die, it is only our flesh, muscles, bones, and organs that die, but the energy goes back to the universe and somebody else will pick it up to develop.

When this energy flows through the body nicely, we are in a state of health. When there is an energetic disturbance in the body, a disease state is created.

Subtle energy runs through the body using a special structure called **energy anatomy**. Our energy anatomy is as specific as our physical anatomy because energetic problems correspond to physical problems. The energetic problems develop in the body first, before physical symptoms become apparent. The energetic problems are possible to pick up when doing a body scan meditation. This alone can prevent a physical illness. To heal, we must correct the energetic problem first. Physical symptoms improve later.

Our Energy anatomy consists of three major elements: **chakras, meridians, and auras.**

The function of energetic anatomy is:

- to collect energetic information from the environment and
- intuitively inform us about everything that is going on inside us and around us.

Our energy system is both a **broadcasting and receiving station.**

**Broadcasting** means that we continuously broadcast information (energy) about ourselves and other people can feel it.

**Receiving station** means that we continuously receive information (energy) from other people and our environment. Also, we receive information from our own organs and body parts. Our Energy system receives and records all this information.

## Let Me Explain Our Energy System

There are three major elements in our Energy system: **chakras, meridians, and auras.**

## Chakras:

**Chakras** are energy centres. You can also call them emotional centres. There are seven major chakras (or energy centres) in the body. Like databanks, chakras collect specific information about our life.

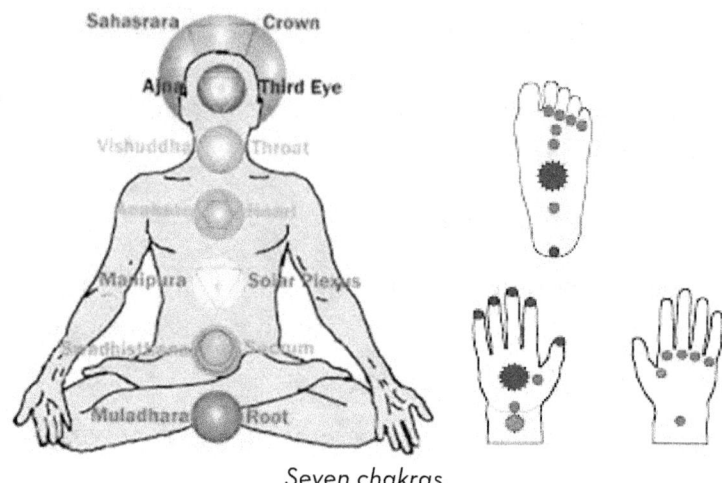
*Seven chakras.*

In addition to the major chakras, we also have minor chakras throughout the body. Minor chakras are located in our hands, feet, armpits, earlobes, inside each organ and inside each anatomical structure of the body.

Minor chakras are used in energy healing and they are as important as major chakras. In fact, minor chakras in our hands are so sensitive that we can do energy healing using our hands.

Your hands help you transmit the energy from one spot to another, clean toxic energy and remove energetic blockages. On the physical level it translates to pain relief, wound healing, stress relief, and transforming negative emotions into positive or neutral.

# Meridians

**Meridians** are energy channels through which the energy flows in the body. Acupuncture and acupressure treatments are based on meridians and their active points. Unless you are an acupuncturist you do not need to learn about meridians. For this reason, we do not discuss meridians in this book.

## Auras

An **Aura** is an energy field around the body – your biofield. Auras are the extension of chakras and have seven colours – the same as chakras. Healthy chakras normally produce healthy auras. With a bit of training, you will be able to see or sense auras. Auras are an important indicator of human health.

# Chapter 4:
# OUR ENERGY CENTRES (CHAKRAS)

In ancient Greece, ancient doctors would go into an altered, dreamlike state and intuitively accessed information about their patients' illnesses. They performed an intuitive body scan on a person instead of using x-rays, MRI or CT scans that we use in modern days. They were very accurate according to some ancient texts. How did they do that? Was it a special talent or a skill?

I researched this and found that they were scanning energy centers (chakras) and organs connected to the chakras. It is called medical intuitive body scan.

## Body scan: A Skill or a Talent?

Each of us can scan our body: it is a skill. Everyone can activate their, 'inner eye' (the ability to see your own organs from the inside – like an x-ray).

Have you heard a common saying, "Nobody knows your body better then you?" This expression is about our 'inner eye' - the ability to connect to our organs and undesrtand them. The reason why some people can't connect to their organs is that from a very young age, they were taught, "Just think with your head." Nobody taught us how to feel and sense.

With practice most people can scan their body. When you understand your own body – you can read other people's bodies too, but do your own healing first.

## I teach People to Scan their Body in Two Ways:

1st **Way:** Scanning the chakras, (connecting to each chakra one by one, sensing the energy inside them, cleansing them and strengthening the chakras).

2nd **Way:** Scanning the body and the organs with your attention, layer by layer, like an x-ray.

Both ways are very powerful and useful for healing and rejuvenating.

Now, let us look at our energy centres (chakras) individually and what they represent.

# The 1st Chakra: The Power of Family and Tribe

### Lesson: All is One (All for One and One for All)

The first energy centre corresponds to the area of the body which touches the earth when a person is seated in a classic cross leg posture of meditation. It connects us to the physical/material world of our

family, and it starts developing right after birth. The energy of our ancestors, the tribal patterns that we call, 'karma,' is here.

Therefore, we are never alone at this level. We 'carry' all our ancestors in the 1st chakra, but it is still a choice how we use this energy – to make us stronger or to keep us weak. Tribal wounds deplete us if we do not become conscious and transform them. All wounds can be healed.

A great example of 'tribal wound' healing is Oprah Winfrey. She had the most difficult childhood. Her mother abandoned her when she was a baby and Oprah lived with her grandmother in segregation. Oprah was physically and sexually abused and fell pregnant at the age of thirteen, giving birth to a stillborn son. As an adult, she managed to transform her wounds into extraordinary strength.

In one of her interviews she was asked, "Oprah do you ever feel uncomfortable, when you come into a room and you are the only black woman in the room?

She answered, "I'm never alone, I carry all my ancestors with me …" This notion gave her so much strength and power, which led her to become one of the most influential women on the planet.

Many people cling to their 'wounds' and let their wounds control their life. The worst things happen when people make excuses for not healing, saying things like, "Because I had problems as a child, I am struggling now." They use the energy of their 1st chakra in a negative way - to weaken them. They do not realise how much power is in the 1st chakra, but they must use it in a positive way - to become stronger, like Oprah did, not the opposite.

On the emotional level, the 1st chakra is responsible for how safe, secure, supported and protected we feel in the world in general. It holds the imprints about security, sexuality, and survival. It is the vortex of energy that urges a person to eat, sleep, to protect him/herself and to be aware of danger. It also contains the energy of our 'inner child' and its traumas, as well as the feelings of fear, rage, and terror that comes from childhood and beyond.

This chakra can be called our Matrix, from which our habits, mindsets and tastes originate, develop, and take form.

Much of people's **life force energy** is kept in the 1$^{st}$ chakra and can either be channelled into fear and stress, or courage and love. It is a choice.

## Medical Intuitive Characteristics of the 1$^{st}$ Chakra

> **Location:** the base of the spine, between genitals and anus.
>
> **Emotional level:** How Safe, Secure, Supported and Protected you feel in the world in general.
>
> **Age of development:** Birth – 5 years old
>
> **Level of Power:** totally external power and is connected to the physical/material world and survival in the tribe.
>
> **Energetic Information Includes:** family relationships, attitudes, family conflicts, family loves and hates, habits, religion, family honour, tribal culture, tribal loyalty, tribal justice, and honour. You are never alone in this chakra. You carry all your ancestors with you in this emotional centre.
>
> **Organs connection:** blood, bones, joints, skin, muscles, legs, feet, anus, and immune system.

## Spiritual & Emotional Characteristics of the 1st Chakra.

> **Gland:** Gonads
>
> **Sense:** Smell
>
> **Element:** Earth
>
> **Personality:** 'I am'
>
> **Balanced Energy:** Centred, grounded, healthy, fully alive, unlimited physical energy, manifesting abundance, master of oneself.
>
> **Excessive Energy:** Egotistic, domineering, greedy, addicted to wealth, indiscriminate use of sexual energy, nervous sexual energy.
>
> **Deficient Energy:** Lack of confidence, not grounded in physical reality, weak, can't achieve goals, self-destructive, feeling unloved or abandoned.
>
> **Colour:** Red
>
> **Crystal to work with:** Garnet and Ruby

## Health problems in the 1st chakra:

Health in the 1st chakra depends on how safe, secure, and supported you feel in the world in general. This sense of security originates from family. If you don't feel supported by your family and friends, then your body will respond by developing 1st chakra problems such as allergies, bones and joints problems, frequent colds, skin issues, chronic fatigue syndrome, fibromyalgia, osteoarthritis, rheumatoid arthritis, Epstein-Barr virus, hepatitis (A, B, or C), mononucleosis, Lyme disease, legs and feet problems, psoriasis or chronic depression.

To develop good health in the first chakra, you need to learn to feel safe with people and learn to balance your own needs with tribal politics. Caring for families and other people consumes time and energy. If you spend more energy taking care of others, than you spend taking care for yourself - you will create an energetic debt, that translates into illnesses and health problems.

For good health you need to give and receive equally. Families should provide you with the sense of support and belonging, otherwise you develop health problems.

NOTE: If you continuously feel unsafe, then, the problem may be yours. You need to look at your own behaviours and how you enable people to act negatively towards you.

The first signs about your sense of safety in a group (family) can be as simple as tiredness, feelings of, 'walking on eggshells,' skin rashes, or aches and pains in the body. These signs let you know that you should change your attitudes and behaviours in the group or leave. If you ignore these warnings, more problems can be developed such as chronic fatigue syndrome, fibromyalgia, back pains, arthritis, frequent infections, allergies, blood, or autoimmune problems.

To maintain health in the 1st chakra organs, you should take yourself home and feel comfortable, safe, secure, and at home in every group and every family. Good affirmation for strengthening the first chakra is: **"I am safe, secure, supported and protected."** Repeat it again and again, anywhere you go, and your sense of safety will improve.

## Emotional Problems of the 1st Chakra.

No money, lack of surviving skills
Not grounded, not practical, no dynamism, no enthusiasm
Internal conflicts, "What I want vs what the family wants"
Not belonging
Fear of living (including suicidal thoughts)
Family conflicts
Tribal wars: "My tribe is better than yours"
Not having stable foundation in life
Lack of physical security
Not being approved of/rejected
Feeling wounded
Feeling abandoned.

## Common Medical Problems Connected to the Tribal Chakra:

**Back pains** show how safe and supported you feel, and what 'burdens' you carry on your back. Look at how you feel about finances and dealing with money. Do you feel lack of support from others? Feeling unloved? Do you hold back love?

**Colon problems** represent holding on to the past. You need to release tribal fears, insecurities, unforgiveness, and feelings of being stuck.

**Constipation and haemorrhoids** represent feelings stuck in the 'same old, same old,' mentality. Stinginess about money and resources. Unconsciously stopping the flow of love and joy. Feeling that change is too difficult.

**Feet and legs problems** imply the feelings of going to a wrong direction. Not feeling that you belong. Wanting to run away.

**Depression, alcoholism, belonging problems** represent the, 'wounded child,' who refuses to heal and just wants to escape. Disconnection from the Divine. Not finding a place to call 'home'.

**Hyperactivity (ADHD)** represents lack of groundedness. Not knowing your place in the world.

**Sleeping problems** represent lack of connectedness to nature and natural rhythms.

**Immune problems, general weakness** represent lack of security in the family. It can come from the feelings of being smothered or overprotected. Feeling not safe in yourself.

**Blood disorders** represent hopelessness and helplessness about family issues. Feeling that, "I have no control over anything."

**Allergies, food intolerances** represent feeling not safe in yourself. Feeling that you are special and not able to connect to others. Look at who you are allergic to – to which person or situation.

**Bone and muscle problems** represent rebelling against authority in your family, groups, or organisations. Taking care of others, because it is expected from you, but not taking care of yourself. Not understanding yourself: your needs, wants and desires.

The spiritual lesson of the 1st chakra is, **'All is One.'** It teaches us to treat each other as one big family and feel safe, secure, and supported in any group or tribe.

## Healing the 1st Chakra Problems

1. Join at least 3-4 groups where you can share your true self and feel that you belong. If one or two fail – you have the support of the others.

2. Do the 1st chakra cleansing and then chakra strengthening with red colour energy (read the chapter, "How to Heal Chakras").

3. Repeat the affirmation for the 1st chakra.
   "I am SAFE, SECURE, SUPPORTED and PROTECTED."

4. During meditation, sense red energy at the base of your spine. Then, spread this red energy throughout your bones, muscles, and skin. Feel the tribal power running through your system.

5. Rooting to the mother Earth exercise: during mediation feel, that roots are growing down from the base of your spine and connecting you to the mother Earth. It helps you feel like you belong to where you are.

6. To feel the tribal energy in your body, you can listen to the national hymn, watch a military parade, watch a group sports game such as soccer, football etc.

7. Start regular exercising until you sweat (at least 3-4 times a week). The tribal chakra is a physical energy chakra. Therefore, you need to be physically active to produce physical energy. Regular exercise builds up the strength in the 1st chakra. I noticed that people's bodies start vibrating with red energy after vigorous workouts.

8. Do Kegel Exercises to strengthen the base muscles. Many doctors recommend Kegel exercises to strengthen the pelvic floor muscles. I noticed that Kegel exercises make the 1st chakra energy stronger and brighter.

   How to do Kegel exercises:
   - Sit down or stand up (either way is good).
   - Squeeze your pelvic floor muscles (as if you are trying to stop the flow of urine).
   - Hold tight and count from 1 to 10.
   - Relax the muscles and count from 1 to 10.
   - Repeat 10 times: tightening and relaxing the base muscles. Do Kegels 3 times a day (morning, afternoon, and night).
   - Feel the strengths coming into your 1st chakra during and after Kegel exercises.

# The 2nd Chakra: The Power of Relationships and Creativity

## Lesson: Honour One Another

The 2nd energy centre, or the sacral chakra, deals with face-to-face, one-to-one relationships and with creativity - our need to create. It corresponds to the pelvic region: sexual organs, bladder, and lower back. It starts developing at about the age of seven,

when children start interacting with people other than family. Here, they begin to develop sensitivity to other people and experience their first, 'fight or flight' response. This chakra absorbs the energy of our early interactions.

Therefore, the sacral chakra manages relationships and everything they represent - love, money, sex, and power. These are the most seductive objects that we have. Everybody loses a lot of energy from this chakra since we all desire these things at some level. It is an expensive chakra to run.

On emotional level it represents our need for relationships and our need to create. We feel this energy in action when we want things, such as: wanting to make money, wanting to make love, wanting to create new things, wanting to learn new things, wanting to develop friendships, wanting to propose a deal etc.

There are a lot of emotions stored in this chakra - negative and positive.

The negative emotions are guilt, shame, blame, control, jealousy, envy, and anger. The positive emotions are the desire to be attractive, appealing, and fascinating, the desire to have loving, fulfilling, passionate, and nourishing relationships, and the desire to create new things and new experiences. We influence others from this chakra – for good or for bad.

Fears of the 2nd chakra:

- Fear of losing control
- Fear of being humiliated, and shamed
- Fear about money (both extremes: greed and poverty mindset)
- Fear related to sexuality and sexual identity.

## Choices and Relationships

The 2nd chakra enables us to make personal choices about relationships and everything they represent. The first time we experience the power of choice as children, at around the age of seven, when we start interacting with people other than family. We go out and start choosing friends, "Should I choose this friend or another friend?"

Before the age of seven, at the level of the tribal chakra, we do not have a choice - our family makes it for us. At the tribal level, we are driven by tribal power or group pressure. There is no individual choice here. Therefore, tribal consciousness is the lowest form of consciousness.

When we move to the 2nd chakra level, we start making choices based on our likes and dislikes and the power of attraction. Here, we realise, that with choices come responsibilities and we learn the lessons that come from relationships.

## Medical Intuitive Characteristics of the 2nd Chakra

**Energy losses:** We lose energy from this centre when we try to control others or allow other people to control us. Also, we lose energy from this centre when we create in a wrong way. For example, many successful women can't fall pregnant because they spend all their creative energy to give birth to their career or business, but when it comes to creating a baby – they can't, because there isn't enough energy left to conceive.

**Location:** Pelvis.

**On an emotional level it represents:** Our desire to have relationships and everything that comes from relationships: money, sex, and power.

**Level of power:** External power - how we use relationships and everything they represent.

**Energetic information includes:** Relationships on personal and business levels. Attitudes to money, sex, and power.

**Organs connection:** Lower back, hips, urinary tract, and sexual/reproductive organs.

## Spiritual & Emotional Characteristics of the 2nd Chakra

**Gland**: Reproductive/sexual glands (male and female glands)

**Sense:** Taste

**Element:** Water

**Personality:** 'I feel,' or, 'I want.'

**Balanced Energy:** Friendly, optimistic, concern for others, sense of belonging, creative, imaginative, intuitive, attuned to your own feelings, sense of humour.

**Excessive Energy:** Emotionally explosive, aggressive, overly ambitious, manipulative, caught up in illusions, overindulgent, self-serving, obsessive thoughts about sex, see people as sex objects.

**Deficient Energy:** Extremely shy, timid, immobilized by fear, overly sensitive, self-negating, resentful, buried emotions, burdened by guilt, distrustful, clinging, guilty about sex, difficulty conceiving, abused, frigid or impotent.

**Colour:** Orange

**Crystal to work with:** Carnelian

## Common Medical Problems Connected to the 2nd Chakra:

**Infertility** means your creative energies go somewhere else – to carer, business, art, sport, relationships etc ... Not enough creative energy to conceive.

**Libido problems** represent feeling uncomfortable as a man or as a woman.

**Bladder problems** means feeling anger towards a partner, being sensitive and vulnerable in relationships, trying to control a partner, or allowing yourself to be controlled by a partner.

**Lack of enjoyment and pleasures – anhedonia** represent the thoughts that, "I can't have any pleasures."

**Problems with youth – longevity and rapid aging** represent the loss of 'the life force' that comes from relationships.

**Lack of charisma** implies that you feel unattractive.

**Partnership problems** represent refusing to understand the lessons that come from relationships. Stuck in a pattern.

**Problems with control (addictions, eating disorders, alcoholism, obesity)** suggest trying to numb the feelings that come from relationships. Relationships with yourself can also be a reason.

**Lower-back pain, hip pain and sciatica** represent feeling insecure about love, money, or both. Feeling that you are, 'not good enough.'

**Urinary, or vaginal infections** represent sexual guilt, feeling "pissed off" with a partner.

**Menstrual-cycle irregularities** represent femininity problems. Having false believes about femininity and what it means to be a woman.

**Fibroids and endometriosis** represent nursing a hurt from a partner (or other people).

**Ovarian cysts: Polycystic Ovary Syndrome (PCOS)** suggest feeling uncomfortable with being a woman.

**Vulvodynia: vulvar vestibulitis** represent fear of opposite sex, thinking that sex is 'dirty.' Shame and guilt about sex.

**Prostate problems: testicular pain** represent feelings not worthy of love, resentful, insecure about being a man.

## Healing the Sacral Chakra:

1. Evaluate your relationships for power games, co-dependency, and control issues.
2. Name three situations where you feel afraid of losing control and try to change it. Mastery of the sacral chakra is achieved by not getting caught by the energy of control.
   **NOTE:** being, 'controlling,' is not only about relationships with others, but also about relationships with yourself. This includes addictions, defensiveness, competitiveness, desire to be first at any cost, righteousness, 'sticking to your guns,' or just feeling tense for no reason at all.
3. Do chakra cleansing and then chakra strengthening with orange energy. (read the chapter, 'How to Heal Chakras').

4. During meditation, sense the energy of your sacral chakra. You can sense it as an orange energy ball inside your pelvis, then spread this energy throughout your body. It brings sexual/creative energy back into your body.

5. Affirmation for the second chakra:
*I am sexy, charismatic, and powerful.*
*I easily attract money and the right people into my life.*

6. Exercise to stay younger and to heal relationships.
During meditation rise energy from your sacral chakra to your heart chakra and back. Feel the energies of these two chakras blend, become one and circulate inside.
This exercise of joining the sacral chakra energy with the heart energy promotes longevity. Also, it helps to heal sexual issues. This exercise was used by monks to channel sexual energy into loving-kindness energy of the heart. You should do it daily for greater benefit.
If you have a partner, both of you should do this exercise daily to clear the sexual energy and blend it with the heart energy.

7. Do Kegel exercises to strengthen the pelvic muscles. Kegels are helpful for strengthening both – the $1^{st}$ and the $2^{nd}$ chakras. Read the steps in 'How to do Kegels,' in the $1^{st}$ chakra healing recommendations.
When your pelvic muscles become stronger – the energy in your $2^{nd}$ chakra becomes stronger, lighter, and vibrant.

# The 3rd Chakra:
# The Personal Power and Self-Esteem

## Lesson: Honour Yourself

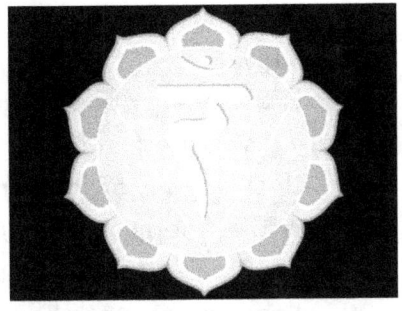

The third energy centre, also known as the solar plexus chakra, begins to develop at puberty. It manages the sense of personal responsibility and self-esteem. Located just above the belly button, it also contains the energy of our stamina, sense of honour, endurance, boundaries, gut instincts, and survival intuition. The solar plexus is the loudest voice in our energetic anatomy because our sense of presence is here. First impressions about people and situations come from this chakra. Then, the impulse spreads over the rest of the body. We call it, 'gut instinct'.

Our success in life depends on the strength of this chakra. It is a part of us that says: "I am going to do what I want to do," and then actually do it. The 'Warrior' archetype is located in this chakra as well as the 'Victim'. It is totally up to you which one you choose to use. Some people use their 'Warrior' archetype often and succeed in everything they do. Some people choose their 'Victim' a lot and stay victims.

The dominant colour of the 3rd chakra is yellow. It looks like your own Sun in the mid-belly and it contains masculine energy.

Other characteristics of the solar plexus chakra energy:

- It is the energy that makes you feel comfortable or uncomfortable in the external world. You see this energy at work and business. I noticed that when people are actively doing things and feel confident about it, they vibrate with yellow energy.
- It is the energy of self-discipline. I noticed that people who are disciplined and who are honest with themselves, vibrate with strong yellow colour.
- It is the energy of taking responsibilities and feeling good about yourself at the same time. Responsible people have yellow aura around them.
- It is the energy of self-worthiness and, "I can do it," attitude. I notice that when people feel, "I am worthy of good things. I can do it." – their aura vibrates yellow.
- It is the energy of strength that helps you overcome challenges: keep persevering under pressure, like a warrior.
- It is the energy that makes you aware about other people's motives: your gut instinct.

The solar plexus is all about your personal strength, courage, self-esteem, honour, personal responsibility, and stamina.

## Medical Intuitive Characteristics of the 3rd Chakra

> **Energy loss:** We lose energy from this centre to our sensitivity to criticisms, self- criticism, not honouring personal boundaries, not keeping your word, not loving yourself and seeing yourself as ugly. Also, when we have fears of rejection, fears of failure, fears that others will discover our secrets.
>
> **Location:** Slightly above and behind the belly button.
>
> **On an emotional level it represents** how much you love and honour yourself. How much responsibility you can take and still feel good about yourself. How much you respect your own boundaries.
>
> **Age of development:** Around puberty when we start developing personal responsibility.
>
> **Level of Power:** External power but partially internalised. It represents how comfortable you feel in relation to others.
>
> **Energetic Information** includes self-esteem and responsibility.
>
> **Organs connection:** Stomach, liver, gallbladder, pancreas, spleen, diaphragm, kidneys, guts, midback and adrenal glands.

## Spiritual & Emotional Characteristics of the 3rd Chakra

**Gland:** Adrenal glands

**Sense:** Sight

**Element:** Fire

**Personality:** 'I can do it'

**Balanced Energy:** Outgoing, cheerful, self-respect, respect for others, strong sense of personal power, have found your gift, able to digest life, able to digest food, skilful, intelligent, relaxed, spontaneous, expressive, take on new challenges, enjoy physical activity, enjoy good food.

**Excessive Energy:** Judgemental, workaholic, perfectionist, overly intellectual, demanding, resentful of authority, a need for drugs to relax, superiority complex.

**Deficient Energy:** Depressed, lack of confidence, worry about what others think, confused, feeling that others control your life, poor digestion, afraid of being alone, need constant reassurance, jealous, distrustful.

**Colour:** Yellow

**Crystal to work with:** Amber, Citrine

## Common Medical Problems Related to the 3rd Chakra:

**Diabetes** (type 2) represents the issues of responsibility and feeling overwhelmed from continuously taking care of others.

**Digestive problems** represent difficulty digesting life, worrying about the future, trying to get more and more of everything when everything is already enough.

**Weight issues** represent protection from other people's energy. Fat grows around the body parts that need protection (read the chapter 'Body Shapes').

**Metabolic problems** represent losing your identity by constantly being of service to others.

**Eating disorders** represent difficulty managing responsibility and self-esteem. Feeling terror, rage, self-rejection. In case of anorexia – denying nourishment.

**Addictions** represent running away from yourself. Not wanting to feel. Escape from life and numbing the pain.

## Self-Esteem and Intuition

People who want to develop their intuition use different techniques to do it - meditation, relaxation, yoga, etc ... But often, spiritual seekers ignore the truth, that intuition is based on self-esteem. Self-esteem is necessary to trust yourself. Without healthy self-esteem, people find it difficult to act on their internal instructions. They doubt, procrastinate, and get distracted from what they need to do.

Self-esteem determines the strengths of our solar plexus where the internal instructions come from. It is called, 'gut instinct'. According to our, 'gut instinct' all other chakras either open up or shut down. If a person feels, "I don't trust myself" – this impulse starts from the solar plexus and goes to the rest of the chakras, making actions impossible.

Strengthening self-esteem improves self-trust and the ability to act on your intuition.

## How to Develop Self-Esteem

- Self-esteem improves when you are actively doing things and seeing the results of your own actions. The more results you can see – the more you trust yourself.
- Make goals and achieve results.
- Do not compare yourself with others. Observe your own progress, 'I am today,' versus, 'I was yesterday,' and take in consideration your own life challenges.
- Change your internal dialog. Always approve of yourself. Believe that you are doing well.
- Always face your own challenges. Do not allow other people to fight your own battles. Only you can do it.
- Be accountable to yourself and practice self-discipline.
- Understand your own weaknesses and strengths.
- Understand your motivations. Who motivates you? Who wants you to do things? To develop self-esteem, you must become a self-motivator. There is no other way.

Self-esteem cannot be developed by doing nothing. Just meditation or relaxation is not enough to improve your self-esteem. The solar plexus is a physical chakra. Therefore, physical energy is necessary to strengthen it – the energy of physical actions.

To test your self-esteem, answer these questions:
- Are you sensitive to criticism?
- Do you criticise yourself?

Answering 'yes' means you need to work on improving your self-esteem. High sensitivity to criticism interferes with your ability to trust yourself. It also makes you feel inferior.

Self-esteem means that you have such a strong sense of self, that external influences do not affect you.

## Healing the Solar Plexus Chakra:

1. To create health in this chakra, you need to learn to balance self-esteem and responsibilities. Are you a responsible person? Do you love and respect yourself? Do you feel worthy?
   Affirmation to heal:
   *"I am confident, strong and courageous. I love and respect myself."*

2. Mastery of the solar plexus is achieved by not getting caught in addictions. Name three addictions that you know are limiting and make a strong effort to stop them. Addictions include emotional eating, sex, over socialising, overthinking, too much shopping, over-exercising, constantly checking phone or emails, Facebook, etc.

3. Practice self-discipline. Self-discipline is the practice of doing what you said you are going to do, even when you do not feel like it.

4. Follow the spiritual lesson of the solar plexus: **Honour Yourself**. That means you love and respect yourself as, 'your own Majesty'.

5. Healing the 3rd chakra requires believing in yourself. The affirmation to heal:
   "*I trust myself. I am worthy of good things. I act on my intuitions.*"

6. During meditation sense yellow energy inside your solar plexus. You can visualise it as your own Sun: strong masculine energy of a peaceful warrior. Spread yellow energy throughout your body and feel strength coming into your body.

7. Do chakra cleansing and then chakra strengthening with yellow energy. (read the chapter, 'How to Heal Chakras').

8. Regular physical activity strengthens the solar plexus. It is still a physical/material energy chakra. Therefore, physical actions are required to build up the energy.

# The 4th Chakra: The Power of Unconditional Love

**Lesson: Love is Divine Power**

The 4th emotional centre, also known as the heart chakra, is located in the chest and it is the centre of unconditional love. I heard it is called the 'mission control,' because love is a driving force of the human soul. Our happiness depends on how much love we can give and receive from others.

The 4th chakra mediates between the lower self, (the 1st, 2nd and the 3rd chakras) and the higher self, (the 5th, 6th and the 7th chakras) and determines their health and strength.

The colour of the 4th chakra is green – like spring leaves and it is associated with the spring season. We start thriving and blossoming with the heart energy. It represents lightness, forgiveness, openness, compassion, and soul connection. Our passion for life is here. The more we develop our connection with the heart chakra, the more fulfilling, sweet, prosperous, joyful, enriched, and warm our lives will be.

Lessons from the heart chakra teach us self-acceptance, self-love, and courage. These are similar to the 3rd chakra lessons but more spiritually enlightened. While the 3rd chakra lessons teach us how to feel about yourself in relationships to others (external power), the 4th chakra lessons teach us how to respond to our own thoughts and feelings (internal power).

External power is the power that can be taken away from you, because it is all about external sources - other people, money, physical possessions, status, jobs etc.

Internal power cannot be taken away from you. It is based on your ability to generate your own energy such as beliefs in your own self-sufficiency. For example, feeling that, "I alone am enough to cope with whatever life throws at me," comes from total self-acceptance and is connected to the internal power. Therefore, the heart chakra is the place where internal power begins.

The 4th chakra energy allows us to create, 'marriages,' which are soulful connections to others. It is not just about romantic relationships, but about all connections with people. The important thing to understand here is that the first and most important marriage you have is the marriage with yourself, because without this marriage, you cannot happily marry others ... Therefore, self-acceptance is the key to opening your heart.

## HEART CHAKRA CHALLENGES:

## Challenge 1: True Forgiveness

People love the heart's energy and often claim that they come 'from the heart'. When you look at them intuitively, you see a different story. The missing component is true forgiveness, which can be difficult, and some people would rather sleep on a bed of hot charcoal then forgive ...

Forgiveness is much more than just saying, "I have forgiven this person ..." Forgiveness is a spiritual act of releasing the wound. After forgiveness, the wound has no authority in your psyche, and it does not hurt you anymore.

### *What is the Difference Between True Forgiveness and Fake Forgiveness?*

For example, if you said, "I have forgiven this person, I don't deal with him anymore, but God knows ... God sees everything." This means that you still want to punish this person. In symbolic terms, you have, "put your weapons down but not the desire to shoot." This is not true forgiveness.

True forgiveness is when you look back and say, "Nothing could have been or should have been any different. Everything is as it should be." Moreover, you are grateful for the lesson. You know that this challenge made you become the person *you are right now*. You love who you are right now – a much stronger and a much better person than you were before the challenge ... This is true self-acceptance, and this is true forgiveness.

Only after true forgiveness you can see your life as a spiritual journey: there is nobody to blame, nothing to regret and everything is as it should be.

If you blame, regret, and feel victimised – you are still in the ego, you are not in the heart. Ego is always painful, hurting, judging, and criticising. Heart forgives. To forgive and release the wound, you need to see what 'good' comes from the situation. Then you can forgive. Read chapter, 'How to Forgive' in this book to learn the steps to forgiveness.

## Challenge 2: Betraying or Compromising in Relationships

Heart energy thrives in relationships, but it is also a prime territory for betraying yourself if you give too much. Compromise is necessary for healthy relationships, because we need to adjust our needs with the needs of others.

### But What is the Difference Between, 'Healthy Compromise,' and, 'Betraying Yourself?'

When you compromise healthily, you say, "Ok, I am doing it for you, and I am doing it out of Love." In a healthy compromise you do not feel that "I have betrayed myself." You feel that you give and receive equally.

When you start to feel that compromising costs you too much energy and you start losing your soul and your heart, then you are betraying yourself.

When you are betraying yourself, you feel the energy of an unhealthy exchange. You feel that you give more than you receive.

Maybe you feel smothered by another person or feel entrapped. This is self-betrayal and this costs you energy and eventually your health.

To have healthy relationships you must be aware of when you are compromising healthily and when you are betraying yourself.

## Challenge 3: Energy Receptivity, Clairsentience

Clairsentience is the ability to sense energy through our hands, body, and organs. People who cannot feel subtle energy will find a blocked heart chakra is often the culprit. It means the more you open your heart through forgiveness and letting go, the more you can sense subtle energy and heal. People who still perceive themselves as wounded, cannot sense energy properly and cannot heal. They must go through forgiveness. Read the chapter about 'Forgiveness' in this book and how to go through forgiveness step by step.

## Medical Intuitive Characteristics of the 4$^{th}$ Chakra

> **Energy losses:** Nothing can drain our energy more than the experiences of a 'broken heart.' To get well, our heart violations must be rectified before the healing even begins. True forgiveness is essential, which includes releasing the wound of any kind.
>
> **Location:** Inside the chest.
>
> **On emotional level it represents** forgiveness and self-acceptance.

**Age of development:** After puberty when we are faced with the challenges of forgiveness and self-acceptance.

**Level of Power:** Internal power. It represents your reactions to your own thoughts, feelings, and experiences.

**Energetic Information includes** the ability to love life with an open heart.

**Organ connections:** Heart and circulatory system, ribs, breasts, thymus gland, lungs, shoulders, arms, hands, diaphragm.

## Spiritual & Emotional Characteristics of the 4th Chakra

**Gland:** Thymus and Lymphatic system.

**Sense:** Touch

**Element:** Air

**Personality:** 'I give and receive love.'

**Balanced Energy:** Physically and emotionally balanced, quality of nurturing, compassion, empathy, friendliness, active in the community, discriminating mind, humanitarian, able to see good in others, able to surrender in a love relationship, healthy use of will power.

**Excessive Energy:** Demanding, overly critical, possessive, moody, martyr complex, loves conditionally, withholds love or generosity, melodramatic, manic-depressive, hyper-tension (especially tension between shoulder blades).

> **Deficient Energy:** Paranoid, indecisive, fear of letting go, fear of being hurt, fear of being free, fear of being abandoned, feelings of unworthiness in love, needing constant reassurance.
>
> **Colour:** Green
>
> **Crystal to work with:** Emerald

## Common Medical Problems Related to the Heart Chakra:

**Heart attacks** represent intimacy issues with others. Wanting to have intimate connections but blocking it due to emotional denial.

**Lung problems** represent emotional porousness and sensitivity, being overwhelmed with emotions. Breathing through, 'emotional clouds.'

**Breast problems** represent issues of nurturing: nurturing others more than nurturing yourself. Treating everybody as 'darling' but crying inside for self-love.

**Shoulder problems** represent 'carrying burdens for others' and an inability to express emotions at a healthy level.

**Arms and hands problems** represent how you handle life situations, embrace life, and how you give and receive Love.

## Healing the 4th Chakra

> 1. Forgiveness process. You need to forgive one person at a time. Read the chapter, 'How to Forgive,' in this book.

2. Remember that the first person who you need to forgive – is yourself. Go through the forgiveness process with yourself. Read the chapter 'How to Forgive,' in this book.

3. Being of service, of true giving: when you give – you receive.

4. Practice generosity as a way of life.

5. On an everyday basis, be aware of creating soulful connections with others rather than having superficial connections.

6. Do the 4$^{th}$ chakra cleansing and then the 4$^{th}$ chakra strengthening with a green colour (read the chapter, 'How to Clean Chakras').

7. Practice the 'Internal smile' exercise daily (read the 'Internal Smile' chapter).

8. Sense the subtle energy inside your organs using Body Scan mediation. Sensing subtle energy inside your body helps to open your heart chakra.

9. Affirmation for strengthening the 4$^{th}$ chakra:
   *"I am loving, kind, compassionate and warm.*
   *I forgive all who have ever hurt me in this or any other lifetime.*
   *I am love, I am love, I am love."*

10. Practice the 'I love you' exercise daily:
    Take a mirror and look into your own eyes. Say, "I love you … *your name* …" Repeat this sentence ten times until you feel the energy of self-love coming into your body. Focus on your heart and feel a loving connection with yourself.

# The 5th Chakra: The Power of Communication and Faith

## Lesson: Surrender Personal Will to Divine Will

The 5th chakra, also known as the throat chakra, is the centre of communication, willpower, and faith. It rules self-expression, the ability to speak your truth, taking responsibility for your own words and making judgements. It gives us the opportunity to say yes or no and helps to develop our confidence and voice. Here, we explore the power to be true to ourselves and act congruently with who we are. Breaking our word or commitment can create emotional and energetic damage in ourselves and others—damage that may affect us for years and lead to disease.

At the level of the 5th chakra, we learn how to make wise choices and take vows. The power of vows can dominate our life and change our life forever. We must have the willpower to be able to take vows and make wise choices. This willpower represents self-control (not controlling others).

To understand willpower, let us look at the evolution of willpower through the chakras.

- At the 1st chakra level, we use willpower to control people in our tribe. For example, a man who controls his family but cannot control himself. This kind of willpower is unhealthy and leads to disease.

- At the 2$^{nd}$ chakra level, we use willpower to control our relationships. For example, a controlling spouse who cannot control his/her own emotions and thoughts. This kind of willpower is unhealthy and leads to disease.
- At the 3$^{rd}$ chakra, we use willpower to control our look and possessions. For example, a person who looks very polished on the outside but feels deeply insecure inside.
- At the level of the 5$^{th}$ chakra, you control nobody but yourself. Your thoughts, your emotions, and your behaviours. At this level we choose what we think and what we feel. We must grow to achieve this level of willpower.

## CHALLENGES OF THE 5$^{TH}$ CHAKRA:

### Challenge 1: Healthy Communication

The throat chakra is the centre of communication and self-expression. People who have problems here can be divided into two extremes: under-assertive and over-assertive. Both extremes are unhealthy and lead to disease. To create health in the 5$^{th}$ chakra we must understand that true communication is **a two-way street** which requires speaking and listening at the same time. We should be able to speak our truth and let other people speak their truth. It also includes being responsible for your own words and promises. Therefore, healthy communication is a two-way street.

### Challenge 2: The Energy of Faith

The throat chakra contains the energy of faith. Faith means complete trust or confidence in something or someone. We express faith (speak what we believe in) through communication. This includes communication with yourself.

Faith is essential for healing. If you do not believe in healing – it is difficult to heal. In fact, it is not possible unless you start believing in it.

Energetically, we all have faith because we all have throat chakras. Even, atheists, people who say, 'I don't believe in anything' – have faith, but they put their faith into a notion that there is no power that helps us or guides us. There are consequences for their beliefs. Some people put their faith into doubt and fear. They believe in doubting everything and have consequences of their faith: Just look at their problems.

When you put your faith into healing – you create healing. Therefore, we must be incredibly careful with the energy of faith. If you do not put it into the right things - it will be re-directed into doubt and fear and create negative results.

## Challenge 3: The Energy of a Wise Choice

The throat chakra helps us to make wise choices. A wise choice is the ability to make a choice and see the consequences of this choice.

To understand the meaning of a wise choice, let us look at the evolution of choice through the chakras.

We start making choices from the level of the $2^{nd}$ chakra, when at the age of seven we start interacting with people other than family. We start choosing friends based on our instincts and the power of attraction. It is an instinctive choice.

As we grow and evolve, we learn to make wise choices. It means we learn to see the consequences of our choices.

Let me explain the difference between a wise choice, (5th chakra) and an instinctive choice, (2nd chakra).

For example: I met a guy and I feel that I am attracted to him. I choose to have a relationship with him straight away, thinking, "I like this guy." This is an instinctive choice, (2nd chakra).

But if I am mature enough, I would think: "Well, my instincts are saying that I like this guy, but what consequences will there be if I have a relationship with him right away?" This is a wise choice, (5th chakra).

Another example: I got a good job offer, and I accept it straight away, thinking that the pay is good. This is an instinctive choice, (2nd chakra).

But if I am mature enough, I would think: "The payment is good, but what will be the consequences on my health, my environment, and my relationships, if I accept this job?" This is a wise choice, (5th chakra) - seeing the consequences of my choice.

All illnesses have connection to the fifth chakra, **because choices are involved in creating all of our experiences**. We begin our life making instinctive choices, then we learn to make wise choices. This is the process of growing and evolving.

## Medical Intuitive Characteristics of the 5th Chakra

> **Energy losses:** Overusing or underusing self-will. Being over assertive or under assertive. Gossiping, bad-mouthing people. Judging, criticising, blaming. Putting your faith in fear. Consciously doing and saying the wrong things. Being chronically indecisive, withholding the truth.
>
> **Location**: throat

**On emotional level it represents** will power and faith.

**Age of development:** As an adult when we learn to speak up and make wise choices.

**Level of Power:** Internal power. It represents your will and your ability to have faith and express it.

**Energetic Information includes** how you communicate and express your truth.

**Organ connections:** throat, neck, thyroid, mouth and all organs inside the mouth including teeth and gums.

## Spiritual & Emotional Characteristics of the 5th Chakra

**Gland:** Thyroid

**Sense:** Hearing

**Element:** Ether

**Personality:** 'I have the power to communicate.'

**Balanced Energy:** Contentment, centred in the present, good sense of timing (can be a good speaker), awareness of time, pleasant voice, good communicator, musically or artistically inspired, expressive and prolific, understanding of spiritual concepts, ability to meditate or experience Divine Energy, sexual energy is used efficiently or may be channelled artistically.

**Excessive Energy:** Self-righteous, overly talkative, dogmatic, or overly religious, addictive tendencies, dominating – sexually and otherwise.

> **Deficient Energy:** Timid, overly quiet, inconsistent, unreliable, loses track of time, devious, inability to express well, conflicts between sexes, nervous.
>
> **Colour:** Blue
>
> **Crystal to work with:** Turquoise, Aquamarine

## Common Medical Problems of the 5th Chakra

**Mouth issues** represent problems with communication in personal relationships. You do not talk and solve your personal disappointments. You find it uncomfortable to discuss what is bothering you in intimate relationships. You feel that such intimate conversations would embarrass you or hurt your pride.

**Neck problems** represent stubbornness, sticking to your opinion and refusing to consider other viewpoints of a situation. The other scenario can be that your communication skills are excellent, but you get very frustrated when your ability to communicate do not solve the problem. The message here is to learn to surrender and accept life as it is.

**Thyroid problems** imply that you are not being able to express what you feel. You do not know how to voice the truth; therefore, you feel stifled while trying to avoid conflict. The 1st chakra is also involved in this problem because family conflicts are the core of the issue.

## Healing the 5th Chakra

1. You must learn to speak your truth.
2. Evaluate your communication style: under-assertive or over-assertive. Become aware of it and try to correct it.
3. Learn to make powerful choices which are congruent with who you are. Become aware when you make powerless choices and correct it.
4. Practice surrendering to the Divine will. At any time, you feel uncertain repeat over and over, "I surrender the outcome to the Divine."
5. Do the throat chakra cleansing with anticlockwise movement and then strengthening it with blue colour energy, (read 'How to Clean Chakras').
6. Singing or chanting for at least 10-20 min a day. Feel the vibrations of your own voice in your body.
7. Develop a healthy routine for yourself. This chakra needs a system to follow. 'Surrendering your will to Divine will,' requires discipline until it becomes a habit.
8. Affirmation for the Throat Chakra:
   "I speak my truth.
   I surrender my Will to Divine will.
   I manage my life with ease and effortlessness."
9. During meditation, sense a blue energy in your throat. Then spread the blue energy throughout your body and around your body. Surround yourself with blue energy. Feel the power coming into your body.

# The 6th Chakra: The Power of the Mind and the Higher-Self Intuition

## Lesson: Seek Only the Truth

The 6th energy centre is also called the 'third eye' chakra. Located in the forehead, it is the centre of wisdom, mind power, higher-self intuition, and the ability to see the truth. It is the centre of the brain, eyes, and ears - the organs that receive information from the world. Their health depends on how you balance this information and how you interpret it. Some people have a tendency to become one-sided and see the world as being too spiritual or too physical. Both extremes are not healthy and create problems in this chakra. Therefore, we should learn to have a flexible mind-set, be comfortable with different views and not be attached to anything.

When open, the 'third eye' allows us to connect to our inner guidance and receive messages from the Divine. Another quality is to help us see the truth and differentiate the truth from illusions. Many people live their life in illusions. Illusions come from the lower chakras: the tribal chakra, relationships chakra, and the relationship with yourself chakra. For example, your tribal beliefs can keep you in illusions for years until you open your, 'third eye,' and see the truth. Your relationships can keep you in illusions when you blindly follow your partners and ignore the truth. Finally, your addictions and temptations can keep you in illusions - you feel that you desire something that is not good for you.

The 'third eye' also contains the higher-self intuition. The higher-self intuition is the ability to foresee something that is not here yet, but you have the ability to materialise it. All inventions are the result of higher-self intuition. This intuition plays an important role in healing because you need to see a new version of yourself first before you create it.

The 'third eye' helps to connect to our organs during the healing process. Connecting to the organs is only possible with a clear, open, and disciplined mind.

Another important aspect here is a symbolic sight. To heal, we must see life symbolically and understand the soul language of life. This is only possible with the fully open, 'third eye.' Our sixth sense (the extrasensory perception) is connected to this chakra also.

## The power of Detachment and Impersonal Mind

The $6^{th}$ chakra contains the energy of detachment and impersonal mind. It is the ability to see life impersonally from an observer point of view, as if you are watching a movie. You do not get emotionally involved in the situations you see; you just observe it.

Impersonal mind and detachment are the best protection from the energy of other people. When you practice detachment, you do not need any protection from the energy of others. You can go anywhere, be with anybody and you are not affected by their energy.

Detachment does not mean you become aloof or stop caring. It means you can silence your own mind from the voices of fear and have such a strong sense of self that external influences do not affect you.

These qualities of the mind are essential for healing because emotional stability is required to heal.

## Medical Intuitive Characteristics of the 6th Chakra

**Energy losses:** Fear of seeing the truth. Denying intuitions and using the mind to twist intuitions. Fear of realistic judgement. Unwillingness to look at and confront your own shadow. Fear to look within and understand your own fears.

**Location:** forehead

**On emotional level it represents** the capacity to see things impersonally, with detachment and beyond emotions.

**Age of development:** As an adult, when we start searching for truth and try to distinguish the truth from illusions.

**Level of Power:** Internal power. It represents how you can change your attitudes and behaviours according to the truth you see.

**Energetic Information includes** how well you see the world, from all possible perspectives.

**Organ Connections:** Brain, eyes, ears, nose, pituitary glands, and nervous system.

## Spiritual & Emotional Characteristics of the 6th Chakra.

**Gland:** Pineal, Pituitary

**Sense:** Thought

**Element:** Energy or Telepathic energy

**Personality:** 'I know who I am'

> **Balanced Energy:** Charismatic, open to guidance, not afraid of death, not attached to material things, can experience telepathy, past lives, or astral travel, self-fulfilled, can be celibate, may have experienced Cosmic Consciousness.
>
> **Excessive Energy:** Proud, religiously dogmatic, tyrannical, demonic.
>
> **Deficient Energy:** Non-assertive, undisciplined, weak-willed, extreme sensitivity to the feelings (energy) of others, afraid of success, schizophrenic.
>
> **Colour:** Indigo
>
> **Crystal to work with:** Azurite and Amethysts

## Common Medical Problems of the 6th Chakra

**Brain disorders** represent twisting intuitions with the mind. Not trusting life. Allow your logic mind to overpower your intuitive mind.

**Eyes problems** represent the ability to balance what you see. Having problems to balance your physical life with how you feel about it.

**Ears problems (deafness and others)** represent your ability to balance what you hear. Having problems with trust: trusting others, trusting yourself and the process of life.

**Nervous system** disorders represent how you take information in and out (release). Being unable to clean yourself from the unwanted energies. Not practicing detachment and impersonal mind.

**Nose problems** represent failure to 'smell the air' – or recognise your own intuitive guidance due to low self-esteem.

To create health in the 6th chakra you should balance the information you receive. It is about balancing spiritual and material, physical and emotional and not going into extremes. Extreme views of life are unhealthy. For example, being too materialistic (physical) or being too spiritual (emotional) – both are unhealthy and will create problems. Being one sided and attached to certain views will create problems in the 6th chakra organs.

You must follow the lesson of this chakra – 'Seek only the Truth,' which means understanding balance in everything you do, feel, or think. Balance is in the middle.

## Healing the 6th Chakra:

1. Practice detachment and impersonal mind.
2. Accept the wholistic approach to health, (not too physical, not too spiritual, but balanced and according to who you are).
3. Understand that everything has meaning. There is nothing to deny or resist but understand.
4. Find a higher meaning from your illness and follow your own path to heal.
5. Evaluate the shadow aspects of your lower chakras: your tribal chakra, your relationship chakra, and your solar plexus power.

6. Practice cleansing your 'third eye' with anticlockwise movements and then strengthening it with indigo colour energy, (read, 'How to Clean Chakras').

7. Practice focused attention and prolonged concentration. To develop the 'third eye' you should be able focus on something for a long time.

   Healing an organ/body part requires your focused attention on the organ until you start sensing energy inside it.

8. Affirmation for healing the 6th Chakra:
   "I follow the Divine plan.
   I am free, and they are free.
   Everything works out for the Highest good.
   All is well."

# The 7th Chakra:
# Our Divine Connection and Life Purpose

### Lesson: Stay in the Present Moment

The seventh energy centre, also known as the crown chakra, is our Divine connection. It is literally our 'grace bank account,' where we receive gracefulness, effortlessness connection to the higher consciousness and the ability to transcend the physical reality.

We can feel the intensity of this chakra energy through meditation and prayer. It is the sense of internal awareness that makes us feel connected with the Divine. Fears related to the physical world are absent here because we feel connected to the universal consciousness at this level.

This is the chakra where the Divine Energy enters our body and then spreads throughout the body. The clearer your 7th chakra, the more life force energy we can receive. This life force energy is also called prana, chi, ki or light.

The criteria for cleanliness and openness of the crown chakra is *our ability to be in the present moment*. Only when we are totally present, we feel connected to the Divine.

## Life Purpose Energy

The crown chakra contains the energy of realising and following our life purpose. Having a purpose helps to recover even from the most 'incurable' illnesses. In fact, all the 'spontaneous remission' cases I have witnessed, were connected to finding a purpose to live.

Many people misunderstand life purpose and confuse it with having a job.

Life purpose is not your job but rather having a reason to live.

Questions like: "Why do I get up each morning? ... What motivates me to live my life? ... What drives me to do what I do?" makes you think about life purpose.

Let me explain this with a real story …

> I met Maria when she was 85 and was diagnosed with stomach cancer. Because of the advanced stage of the illness, doctors refused to operate, and she was sent home to die. She lived alone and had no family. Originally, she came to Australia from Russia with her two sons, but they both died. She also had two sisters who also died. She was totally alone, in a foreign country and had an incurable illness.
>
> She was devastated … But her intuition guided her to go to the RSPCA (animal welfare organisation) and adopt five homeless cats. She started caring for these cats in her own house. When I met her, she told me, "Irina, I get up each morning because my babies need me. What happens to my babies if I don't get up each morning?" This was her purpose to live.
>
> Last time I met Maria she was 90, five years after the diagnosis. She did the same things – looked after her cats. When I asked her, "Maria, what about your illness?"
>
> She replied, "What illness, darling?"
>
> I said, "You had a cancer, remember?" She answered, "Oh, doctors said I had, but I don't even think about it anymore." ….

> Her healing experience is related to the 7$^{th}$ chakra phenomenon called, 'blessing in disguise,' or, 'divine paradox.' It happens when the Universe takes away everything from you on the physical level in order for you to connect to the spiritual.
>
> I often think, what would have happened if her family members were still alive? Everything would be different. Her sons would have probably allocated a bed for her and hired a nanny to look after her. She would have had only one choice – lay in bed and be sick. Most likely, she would have died after a few months – this was what doctors said.

## Prophetic Intuitions

When this chakra is open, a person can see and understand the deepest mysteries of life. At this level, the life force flows into our body, allowing us to look into past lives and see our soul's history.

Prophetic intuitions come from the crown chakra. It happens when a person can foresee a better future for many people, maybe for the whole nation, and then take the whole nation to a better future. People like Nelson Mandela, Mother Teresa and the Dalai Lama had this kind of intuition. It is all about connecting to the collective consciousness, receiving information, and then using this information for the higher good of all people. Not everybody can have prophetic intuitions, only some people can.

## Inspirations

All inspirations, be it about a new project or creating a 'new me' come from the crown chakra and then they spread throughout the body. A powerful feeling, "I can do anything," comes from this chakra, but of course, we need to use the power of our lower chakras, to bring our inspirations into reality. This is why many people receive inspirations but cannot materialise them. It is difficult for them to work with the lower chakras' energies, the tribal power, relationships power and the relationship with yourself. A lot of work and dedication are needed to overcome the resistance of the lower chakras' energy.

## 'Dark night of the soul'

The dark night of the soul is a time when we experience a difficult and significant transition into a deeper meaning and devotion. It is a period of deep confusion, isolation, meaninglessness, and dissatisfaction with the existing life. During the 'dark night', our soul is searching for higher meaning and devotion. This period can last from 3 month up to 1 year and is purely connected to the development of the crown chakra.

It often occurs when someone reaches the time in life that requires full surrendering to Divinity.

A middle age crisis is in this category, when people start feeling meaninglessness in their so called, 'normal life' and crave for deeper meaning, devotion, and higher values. We need these periods. They are difficult to overcome but the result is good and empowering. New stages of life start from the 'dark nights of the soul.'

I believe that depression is a spiritual crisis. People enter their 'dark night of the soul' and cannot come back from it. Their soul is searching for higher meaning and devotion - not for antidepressants.

## Medical Intuitive Characteristics of the 7th Chakra

> **Energy losses:** The greatest energy losses in this chakra come from the feelings of hopelessness and helplessness.
>
> **Location:** the crown of the head.
>
> **On emotional level it represents** recognising and following your life purpose.
>
> **Age of development:** As adults when we crave for higher meaning and purpose.
>
> **Level of Power:** Internal power. It is our ability to be present and connected to the Divine at every single moment of life.
>
> **Energetic Information includes** the Divine energy. It can also be called prana, ki, chi, light, or life force.
>
> **Organ connections:** Entire nervous system, musculoskeletal system, and skin.

## Spiritual & Emotional Characteristics of the 7th Chakra

> **Gland:** Pituitary and Pineal
>
> **Sense:** Divine Compassion
>
> **Element:** Subtle Energy (Prana, chi, ki, life force)
>
> **Personality:** 'I surrender to Divine Will'
>
> **Balanced Energy:** Open to the Divine, able to work miracles, can transcend the laws of nature, access to the unconscious and subconscious, realisation of immortality, awareness of death and re-birth.

> **Excessive Energy:** Constant sense of frustration, unrealised power, psychotic, manic-depressive, frequent migraine headaches, destructive, sexual expression ranging from passionate to distant.
>
> **Deficient Energy:** Loss or lack of joy, catatonic, complete inability to make decisions, uncommunicative.
>
> **Colour:** White and violet
>
> **Crystal to work with:** Quartz and Diamond

## Medical problems of the 7th Chakra:

The 7th chakra problems can begin in any organ but progress to their extremes. For example, lung problems are related to the 4th chakra but life-threatening lung cancer, or degenerative lung disorders such as emphysema or severe asthma fall into both - the 4th and the 7th chakras. Mild arthritis is related to the 1st chakra, but severe and chronic arthritis fall into both – the 1st and the 7th chakras. Any illnesses that become chronic or life threatening are connected to the 7th chakra.

The most dangerous emotions that turn mild illnesses into degenerative and chronic are hopelessness and helplessness. Overcoming these are necessary to heal any illness.

Finding a life purpose and a greater sense of devotion is a sure way to overcome hopelessness and helplessness. Read Maria's story again – a cat lady who found her life purpose at the age of 85 and healed her, 'incurable' illness.

## Chapter 5:
# THE SPIRITUAL DESIGN

Our energy anatomy represents our spiritual design. Each energy centre (chakra) has a lesson which we must learn to stay well and healthy.

These are the seven spiritual lessons encoded in the chakras:

1. All Is One
2. Honour One Another
3. Honour Yourself
4. Love Is Divine Power
5. Surrender Personal Will to Divine Will
6. Seek Only the Truth
7. Live in the Present Moment.

According to spiritual design, if we live our life following these seven spiritual truths, we should live at least 120 years, and stay healthy. Some research suggest that we should live even up to 130-150 years and stay healthy. Recently, Harvard University professor and molecular biologist David Sinclair publicly stated that human cells can regenerate themselves forever if nothing stops or blocks the process of cell's regeneration and this has been proven in the Petri dish.

In real life, we do not see many people living up to 120 years and nobody dies from old age. People die from diseases. They die from infections, cancers, dementia, organs failure etc. Our life span is shortened by diseases which are energetic losses to different issues of our life. To heal, we need to bring this energy back into our body and restore our biofield. Antient spiritual traditions call it, 'claiming your spirit back.'

One way to, 'claim your spirit back', is to do a chakra scan meditation daily. When you scan your own chakras, you become aware of the energetic losses to different issues of your life, then you can stop the losses and restore your energy. You should do it daily, preferably, before going to bed. Here are the steps to do it.

## Chakra Scan Meditation

### The 1st Chakra.

Focus your attention on the 1st chakra and take a few deep breaths. When you exhale, push the air through the 1st chakra, as if you are breathing through it. Visualise this chakra as a red ball of energy, rotating clockwise. Feel the sensations in this area. You may sense tingling or crawling sensations, which are the subtle energy in this chakra.

Now connect to the emotional information kept in the 1st chakra.

Through this emotional centre you are connected to all people in your life. Ask yourself, "Have I been true to the 'All is one' principle, treating everybody as if we are one?" To restore your power here, you need to bless your family, your culture, your place of birth and honour your sacred agreements with them. Feel the strength coming into your body when you do this.

If you do not feel strength coming into your body when honouring your families, then you need to ask yourself why and remedy it. Your sense of safety depends on this connection. Go to the chakra's questions to help you understand and correct it. You need to feel safe in order to heal.

## The 2nd Chakra

Focus your attention on the 2nd chakra. Take a few deep breaths and when you exhale push the air through the 2nd chakra, as if you are breathing through it. Visualise this chakra as an orange ball of energy rotating inside your pelvis. Feel the orange energy spreading through your pelvis. Feel it as a tingling and crawling sensations and remember that it is a sensual experience not a logic one.

Now connect to the emotional information kept in your pelvis. This area collects information about your relationships and creativity. Creativity is not just about artistic abilities, but it is about how you create life in general. Everything in life is a product of your creativity including your problems. Do you over-create in one area and under-create in another? Maybe you put all your energy into work but compromise your health? Or maybe you put all your energy in relationships but compromised yourself. Bless all your creations, work, and projects ... Bless your relationships, personal and professional and honour the lessons you learned from them ... Feel the energy coming into your body when you are blessing your relationships and creations.

If you do not feel power coming into your body when honouring your relationships and creativity, then you need to ask yourself why and remedy it. Go to the chakra's questions to help you understand and correct it. You need to balance your relationships and creativity to stay healthy.

## The 3rd Chakra

Focus your attention on the 3rd chakra (solar plexus) and take a few deep breaths. When you exhale, push the air through your solar plexus, as if you are breathing through it. Visualise this chakra as a yellow ball of energy inside your upper belly. Feel sensations in this area. You may sense tingling or crawling sensations, which are the subtle energy of this chakra.

Now connect to the emotional information kept in your solar plexus. This chakra collects energies such as how you feel about yourself. You need to evaluate your self-esteem and your sense of responsibility. Have you compromised yourself? Have you been responsible and behaved according to your standards? Do you like yourself?

To feel strong in this chakra, you need to respect yourself and feel respected. Visualise yellow colour energy coming into your solar plexus. Allow this energy to spread in your belly. This is the energy of self-respect and honour. Feel it.

If you do not feel power coming into your body when honouring yourself, then you need to evaluate why and correct it. Go to the chakra's questions to understand and correct it. You need to honour yourself to stay healthy in this area.

## The 4ᵗʰ Chakra

Focus your attention on the 4ᵗʰ energy centre (heart chakra) and take a few deep breaths. When you exhale push the air through your heart chakra, as if you are breathing through it. Visualise this chakra as a green ball of energy in your chest and feel green vibrations there. You may feel it as a tingling and crawling sensation in your chest.

Now connect to the emotional information kept in your heart chakra. This chakra collects information about unconditional love - or how much you love life, yourself, and other people. True forgiveness is required to feel this kind of love. You may receive messages about who you need to forgive and what you need to let go of. You may have urges to forgive right now. Follow your heart's desires and do what is required. Then, bless all your relationships, bonds, and marriages. Recognise that the first and most important marriage you have is the marriage with yourself, because without this marriage, you cannot happily marry others.

If you do not feel power coming into your body when blessing your relationships and marriages, then you need to ask yourself why and correct it. Go to the chakra's questions to help you understand and correct it. You need to love your life unconditionally in order to heal and stay healthy in this area.

## The 5ᵗʰ Chakra

Focus your attention on the 5ᵗʰ chakra - the throat area. Take a few deep breaths. When you exhale, push the air through your throat, as if you are breathing through it. Visualise this chakra as a blue ball of energy in your throat and feel blue vibrations there. You may sense it as tingling or crawling sensations in your throat.

Now connect to the emotional information kept in your throat. This chakra collects information about how you communicate and express yourself. Evaluate your words when you talk to people. If you expressed harmful words, send them love. Remember that true communication is a two-way street. You need to be able to speak your truth and listen to people at the same time. Bless the way you speak and feel the energy of the, 'right speech,' coming into your body as blue energy.

If you do not feel power coming into your body when blessing your, 'right speech,' then evaluate why and correct it. Go to the chakra's questions to understand it. You need to communicate effectively and express yourself clearly to be healthy in the throat area.

## The 6$^{th}$ Chakra

Focus your attention on the 6$^{th}$ chakra's forehead area. Take a few deep breaths. When you exhale, push the air through your forehead, as if you are breathing through it. Visualise this chakra as an indigo ball of energy in your forehead and feel the indigo vibrations there. Now connect to the emotional information kept in your 6$^{th}$ chakra. This chakra reflects your wisdom and ability to see the world from all different perspectives. It shows your ability to see the truth and practice detachment and impersonal mind. To be healthy in this area you need to see your own path and your place in life. This is your truth. Bless your path and bless your truth. Feel the power coming into your body as an indigo energy when doing that.

If you do not feel power coming into your body, then evaluate why you cannot see your own path and correct it. Go to the chakra's questions to help you understand and correct yourself. You must see your truth to maintain health in this area.

## The 7th Chakra

Focus your attention on the 7th energy centre, the crown chakra. Take a few deep breaths. When you exhale, push the air through the top of your head, as if you are breathing through it. Visualise this chakra as a brilliant crown or a halo at the top of your head.

Now connect to the emotional information kept in the 7th chakra. This chakra connects you with the energy of purpose, grace, and oneness with the Universe. It is about your ability to be present and feel Divinely connected.

Bless the present moment now and realise your Divinity. Feel the power coming into your body when you connect to the present moment. If you do not feel energy coming into your body when connecting to the present moment, ask yourself why and correct it. Go to the chakra's questions and evaluate yourself. To heal yourself and stay healthy you must follow the spiritual truth, 'Stay in the present moment' – the lesson of the 7th chakra.

You should do the Chakra Scan meditation daily. It will allow you to assess your health and restore your energy level. It also helps to develop a skill to scan your body. When you learn how to scan your own body, you can scan the energy of other people.

## Reading Energy on Other People

I thoroughly recommend that you learn reading your own energy field first before you read other people's energy. When people interact, their auras connect. You share with people your energy and they share with you theirs. Understanding your own energy helps to share a better energy with others.

Energy reading on other people is the same process as reading your own energy. You scan their chakras and the relevant organs.

To learn about the energetic meaning of organs and the emotional meaning of symptoms, read my book, "The Secret Energy of Your Body: An Intuitive Guide to Healing, Health and Wellness."

# Chapter 6:
# CHAKRA'S QUESTIONS

After reading and understanding what each chakra represents and what role chakras play in health and well-being, you are now ready for a self-test. Answering the chakra's questions helps to understand your health right now. There are two parts for each chakra: Physical health questions and Emotional health questions. Each question touches specific details about your life which you need to know in order to heal and be well.

Take a pen and paper and answer all the questions one by one.

## The 1st Chakra (The Tribal Power)

### Physical Health checklist:

1. Do you have bone problems such as arthritis, osteoporosis, or back problems?
2. Are you prone to accidents? Broken bones?
3. Do you have blood problems such as anaemia or bleeding disorders?
4. Do you often get sick with flu and colds?
5. Do you suffer from fatigue?

6. Do you have psoriasis, eczema, acne, or other skin disorders?
7. Do you have haemorrhoids, constipation, or colon problems?
8. Do you have autoimmune illnesses?
9. Do you have allergies?

Answering 'yes' to any of these questions means, that you have some issues with the 1st chakra – about how safe, secure, supported and protected you feel in the world in general. You need to do chakra cleansing and chakra strengthening to heal it. Read how to do chakra cleansing and chakra strengthening in the relevant chapters in this book.

## Emotional Health checklist:

1. List all the blessings that came from your family.
   *(Note! if you have difficulty counting blessings, then, look at the lessons you learnt from overcoming the challenges presented by your family).*
2. List all the blessings that came from your culture and the place of your birth.
3. What positive things did you learn from your father?
   *(Note! If you have difficulties answering this question, then acknowledge all the lessons that came from your father).*
4. What positive things did you learn from your mother?
   *(Note! If you have difficulties answering this question, then acknowledge all the lessons that came from your mother).*
5. Do you attract partners that are like your mother or father? What are their traits? Have you tried to change the negative patterns?

6. In personal relationships, do you feel that you re-create the situations you remember your parents had with each other? Name these situations.
7. Is there a karmic pattern in your life that is repeated, again and again?
8. Do you have any unfinished business with your family members? Have you tried to heal it?
9. Do you manage the tribal politics at work, social groups, or friend's group? Or this is still a challenge?
10. Do you feel nervous when things change?
11. What tribal characteristics do you generally like in people? Do you cultivate them in yourself?
12. Do you have trouble feeling loved by an independent person?
13. What superstitions do you have that still have power over your psyche?
14. Do you feel superior or inferior when you are with other people? Did you try to heal it?

Answering these questions helps to evaluate the 1st chakra emotional patterns that are hidden from your awareness. These emotional patterns need to be corrected in order to heal. Practice positive affirmations to change the thought pattens from negative to positive.

## The 2nd Chakra
## (The Power of Relationships and Creativity)

### Physical Health checklist:
1. Do you have problems with sexual/reproductive organs?
2. Do you have infertility problems?

3. Do you have low back pain or sciatica?
4. Do you have coccyx or pelvic pains?
5. Do you have bladder issues or problems with urination?
6. Do you worry about getting old (aging)?
7. Do you have female or male hormonal problems?
8. Do you have addictions?
9. Do people say that you have a lack of charisma?

Answering 'yes' to any of these questions means, that you have some issues with the 2$^{nd}$ chakra – how you balance your creativity, relationships, and work (money). You need to do chakra cleansing and chakra strengthening to heal it. Read the relevant chapters in this book - how to do chakra cleansing and strengthening.

### Emotional Health checklist:
1. How do you feel about your creativity? Are you able to materialise your ideas?
2. Are you competitive? Do you thrive on competition/deadlines?
3. Do you feel that you always need to push hard to survive at work or in relationships?
4. Do you have co-dependency issues in your relationships?
5. Do you gossip? Do you embellish, 'facts' to make things, 'more interesting?'
6. Are you comfortable with your sexuality? If not, did you try to heal it?
7. Do you use people for sexual pleasure or money? Have you felt used?
8. Can you speak up about your sexual boundaries?

9. Can you speak about money in a neutral/non-emotional way?
10. Do you play power games in relationships: Stalking your partner, checking their emails, phone messages etc?
11. Do you compromise important things for the sake of financial security?
12. Do you make choices based on survival fears?
13. Do you often feel guilty?
14. Do you feel comfortable about your body?
15. Do you have problems with being overindulgent? Have you tried to heal it?

Answering these questions helps to evaluate your emotional patterns which need to be corrected in order to heal. Use positive affirmations to counteract each negative pattern.

# The 3rd Chakra (The Power of Self-Esteem and Responsibility)

## Physical Health checklist:
1. Do you have digestion problems, such as a peptic ulcer, mouth problems, oesophagus, stomach, small intestines, large intestines (or colon) or rectum problems?
2. Do you have hepatitis or other liver and gall bladder problems?
3. Do you have spleen problems?
4. Do you have metabolic problems such as diabetes, adrenal gland problems, pancreatitis or other issues with blood sugar and hormones levels?
5. Do you have problems with addictions?

6. Do you have 'body image' problems?
7. Do you have weight issues such as obesity?
8. Do you have anorexia, bulimia or a binge eating disorder?
9. Do you suffer from indigestion or acid reflux disorder?

Answering 'yes' to any of these questions means, that you have some issues with the $3^{rd}$ chakra – how you balance your self-esteem and responsibility. You need to do chakra cleansing and chakra strengthening to heal it. Read the relevant chapters in this book how to do chakra cleansing and strengthening.

## Emotional Health checklist:

1. Do you like yourself? If not, have you tried to heal the problems?
2. Do you attract people who have addictions?
3. Have you been called 'needy' in relationships?
4. Do you criticise yourself? Do you criticise others?
5. Do you have uncontrollable habits such as eating, drinking, smoking, shopping, or overexercising that you use to 'calm' yourself?
6. Do you need approval of others to act on your internal instructions?
7. Are you comfortable to admit when you are wrong? Can you accept a constructive feedback without feeling defensive?
8. Do you feel responsible for everyone but have no time to take care for yourself?
9. Do you respect yourself?
10. Do you follow through with your decisions?

11. Would you stay in a relationship with a person you do not love for survival reasons, such as loneliness or economic reasons etc?
12. Do you know your boundaries in relationships? Do you allow people to violate them? Do you violate other people's boundaries?
13. Are you aware of the intentions of other people? Do you allow yourself to be used? Or do you use other people for security reasons?
14. Do you see yourself as a strong person or a weak person? What are the reasons for that?

Answering these questions helps to evaluate the 3$^{rd}$ chakra emotional patterns that you may not be aware of. These emotional patterns need to be changed to heal. Use positive affirmations to counteract each negative pattern.

# The 4$^{th}$ Chakra (The Power of Unconditional Love)

## Physical Health checklist:
1. Do you have problems with your heart, arteries, or blood vessels?
2. Have you had a heart attack?
3. Do you have high blood pressure?
4. Do you have high cholesterol problems?
5. Do you have lung issues such as asthma, bronchiectasis, emphysema or other?
6. Do you have any breast problems such as lumps, cysts, or cancer?

7. Do you have shortness of breath or chest tightness?

Answering 'yes' to any of these questions means, that you have some issues with the $4^{th}$ chakra – how much you can forgive and love unconditionally. You need to do chakra cleansing and chakra strengthening to heal it. Read the relevant chapters in this book - how to do chakra cleansing and strengthening.

## Emotional Health checklist:
1. Do people call you, 'too sensitive,' or 'too emotional?'
2. Do you cry easily?
3. Do you have relationships that still need healing?
4. Do you have emotional memories that still need healing? What have you done to heal them?
5. Have you ever used your wounds to emotionally connect to people? Do you have 'wound-mates?'
6. Are you aware of the situations when you become controlled by the wounds of another person? What actions did you take to stop this control?
7. Do you have anybody to forgive? What are the reasons for not being able to forgive?
8. Do you need to forgive yourself?
9. Do you have fears that if you become emotionally healthy you will not need intimate relationships?
10. Do you associate intimate relationships with sharing the 'wound?'
11. Do you have relationships based on, 'keeping the wound alive?'
12. What is your definition of 'unconditional love?' Does it include self-love and self-acceptance?

13. Do you often avoid people because you feel overwhelmed by emotions?
14. Have you felt not worthy of love, especially regarding intimate relationships? What steps have you taken to heal it?
15. Do you allow yourself to receive kindness by accepting both giving and receiving in a gracious way?

Answering these questions helps to evaluate your emotional patterns in the 4th chakra which need to be healed. Do positive affirmations to change the thought pattens from negative to positive.

## The 5th Chakra
## (The Power of Communication and Willpower)

### Physical Health checklist:
1. Do you have mouth, gums, or teeth problems?
2. Do you have thyroid problems?
3. Do you have jaw problems such TMJ disorder, locked jaw etc?
4. Do you have neck problems?
5. Do you often get tonsillitis, laryngitis, or a sore throat?
6. Do you have root canal problems in your teeth?

Answering 'yes' to any of these questions means, that you have some issues with the 5th chakra – how well you communicate and express yourself. You need to do chakra cleansing and chakra strengthening to heal it.

## Emotional Health checklist:
1. Do you consider yourself to be a 'strong-willed' person? Why do you think this way?
2. Do you allow other people to make choices for you? Do they control your will power?
3. Do you try to control the choices of another person?
4. Are you over-assertive or under-assertive?
5. Do you have people around you who are over-assertive or under-assertive? Do you see the personal match?
6. Do you express your needs, wants and desires easily?
7. Can you speak what is bothering you in intimate relationships without feeling embarrassed or humiliated?
8. Do you listen to your partners and encourage them to speak their 'truth'?
9. Are you honest with yourself? Do you keep your word?
10. Do you trust the Divine guidance? If not, then, who and what do you trust?'
11. Are you aware of the situations in which you procrastinate to take actions, but you know that it is only up to you to do it?
12. Do you blame, criticise, or badmouth people?
13. Do you tell lies to mislead others?
14. Do you use negative language to express yourself? Do you minimise yourself?
15. Do you find that it is easier for you to communicate with the spiritual world and animals, rather than talk to people?
16. Do you become upset, even devastated, when your attempts to communicate with someone fails?
17. Can you easily accept the attitude, "I surrender the outcome to the Divine"?

Answering these questions helps to evaluate your emotional patterns which you need to heal. Use positive affirmations to counteract each negative pattern.

# The 6th Chakra (The Power of the Mind)

## Physical Health checklist:
1. Do you have frequent headaches or migraines?
2. Do you have insomnia or other sleeping disorders?
3. Do you have memory problems or dementia?
4. Do you have eye problems: bad vision, macular issues, cataracts etc?
5. Do you have hearing problems or illnesses in the ears?
6. Do you suffer from dizziness or balance problems?

Answering 'yes' to any of these questions means, that you have some issues with the 6th chakra – how openly you see the world from all different perspectives. You need to do chakra cleansing and chakra strengthening to heal it.

## Emotional Health checklist:
1. Have you been called, 'scatterbrain' or your mind is always in the clouds?
2. Is learning new things difficult for you?
3. Do you often complain that you cannot understand technology, computers or have problems navigating websites?
4. Do you still consider yourself 'wounded' from the past experiences and cannot change your thoughts about it?
5. Do you have problems with seeing things symbolically?

6. When a friend talks about personal problems, can you see a situation from an impersonal point of view?
7. Do you often feel defensive and protect your old views which you know are not true anymore?
8. Do you have dreams? Can you interpret your dreams in a positive and constructive way?
9. Can you be an 'observer' in a stressful situation to 'see the truth?'
10. Are you afraid of the changes that pursuing your highest potential brings?
11. Do you still have negative behaviours that you cannot control? What are these behaviours?
12. Do you judge people? Do you judge yourself?
13. What excuses do you make to justify your negative behaviours?
14. Have you defined your own path to which you can commit and feel devoted to?
15. Do you feel the difference between connecting to your Higher Self and to your Lower Self? Define the differences.

Answering these questions helps to evaluate your emotional patterns which you need to heal. Use positive affirmations to counteract each negative pattern.

## The 7th Chakra (The Power of Divine Connection)

### Physical Health checklist:
1. Do you have a chronic illness such as depression, severe anxiety, chronic fatigue, fibromyalgia, and the like?

2. Do you have cancer or other illnesses that are considered 'incurable?'
3. Do you feel that you, 'can't get out of bed' most of the time?
4. Do you have a serious neurological illness?
5. Do you have an illness that is continuously deteriorating?

Answering 'yes' to any of these questions means, that you have some issues with the 7$^{th}$ chakra – how connected you are to your life purpose and having reasons to live. You need to do chakra cleansing and chakra strengthening to heal it.

## Emotional Health checklist:
1. Do you know reasons why you get up each morning? Name these reasons.
2. What is your definition of a life purpose?
3. Are you a workaholic and define your life purpose with having a job?
4. Do you feel that you 'lost' your life purpose by wandering around and trying things rather than committing?
5. Do you pray for Divine guidance? What answers do you receive?
6. When you pray, do you pray to get more physical stuff such as more money, relationships, houses etc. or do you pray with gratitude and appreciation?
7. Have you defined your spiritual path? Do you feel that your spiritual path is better than other people's paths?
8. Do you meditate daily?
9. Can you sense the 'subtle energy' inside your body? Do you practice sensing subtle energy daily?

10. Can you energetically connect to your organs? Describe the feelings.
11. In which areas of your body do you resonate with your truth?
12. Do you practice living in the present moment and not getting caught up in the past or future?
13. Are you afraid of surrendering to the Divine because of the loss of control you think it brings?

Now you have evaluated your current situation and can see what things you need to heal.

## How to interpret this test?

The Physical Health checklists pinpoint which chakras need your attention to heal. Healing means removing negative energy from the chakras and then strengthening the chakras with positive energy. In the next chapter, you can learn how to clean chakras from negative energy and then how to put positive energy into the chakras.

The Emotional Health checklists pinpoint the emotional patterns that you need to heal. It means consciously changing the old negative patterns and accepting new positive patterns instead. Use positive affirmations to change your negative patterns.

## Chapter 7:
# HOW TO HEAL CHAKRAS

Each chakra can be healed. Chakra healing consists of:
1. Cleansing (removing toxic energy from the chakras)
2. Strengthening (putting positive energy into the chakras)

Both techniques, cleansing and strengthening, are performed by using your hands. Your hands can heal you. It is not just about laying hands on the body but about sensing energies and working with energies.

## How to do Chakra Cleansing (energy out)

1. Sit comfortable in a chair. Relax and take a few deep breaths.
2. Put your hands together and rub them until they are warm.

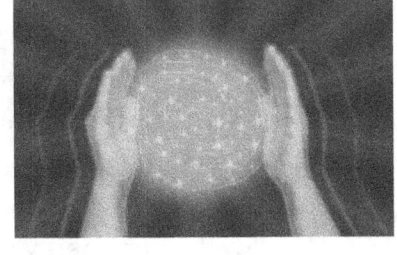

3. Spread your hands apart 20-25 cm and feel the 'energy ball'. You feel it by sensing 'tingling and crawling' sensations in your hands. It means your hands are ready to sense energy.

4. Bring your right hand, if you are righthanded, 20-25 cm from your first chakra (from the front). Focus on your 1st chakra by visualising a red ball of energy rotating at the base of your spine.
5. With your hand find the edge of your 1st chakra aura (from the front). You feel it as resistance or 'tingling' sensations.
6. Start anticlockwise movement with your hand as if you are scooping ice-cream from the bucket. To understand the direction, put a watch on your body, face up and see which way is anticlockwise.

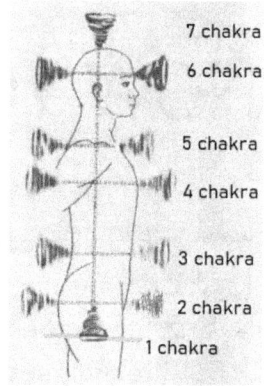

7. When you do anticlockwise movements, you feel as if you are collecting 'dust'. Throw this 'dust' in the fire (a burning candle). You must burn this negative energy. If you throw the 'dust' in the room, the negative energy will come back to you or somebody else will pick it up.
8. Keep cleansing the 1st chakra with anticlockwise movements until you feel lighter or follow the two minute per chakra rule.
9. Move higher to the 2nd chakra and repeat the process. Visualise an orange ball of energy in your pelvis and clean it with anticlockwise movements. Always throw the toxic energy in the fire.
10. Move to the 3rd chakra and follow the same steps. Visualise a yellow ball of energy in your upper belly. Clean it until you feel lightness or follow the two minute per chakra rule.

11. Move to the 4$^{th}$ chakra and feel a green ball of energy in your chest. Repeat the steps.
12. Move to the 5$^{th}$ chakra and feel a blue ball of energy in your throat. Follow the same process of cleansing.
13. Move to the 6$^{th}$ chakra and feel an indigo ball of energy in your forehead area. Follow the same steps.
14. Move to the 7$^{th}$ chakra and feel brilliant colour energy at the top of your head. Clean it with anticlockwise movements until you feel lighter.

It takes about 15 -20 min to clean all seven chakras. It can take longer if you feel that energetic contamination is strong.

After a sufficient cleansing you can start strengthening your chakras.

Always do cleansing first. All chakras need to be cleaned before you put energy in the chakras.

## How to do chakra strengthening (energy in)

1. Rub your hands together until they are warm. Spread your hands 20-25 cm apart and feel the 'energy ball' in your hands. This is your subtle energy.
2. Visualise a red light entering the space between your hands. Now you hold a 'red ball' of energy. Feel the red vibrations.
3. Bring this 'red ball' of energy to your 1$^{st}$ chakra and start clockwise movements with your hand.
4. Feel red energy spreading through your 1$^{st}$ chakra and its organs.
5. Now move to the 2$^{nd}$ chakra and repeat the process. Rub your hands together again, spread them apart, feel the

energy ball. Visualise an orange light entering the space between your hands. Hold the 'orange ball' and then bring it to your $2^{nd}$ chakra. Start clockwise movements with your hands to instil the orange energy into your $2^{nd}$ chakra.

6. Repeat the same process for each chakra, generating yellow energy for the $3^{rd}$ chakra, green energy for the $4^{th}$ chakra, blue energy for the $5^{th}$ chakra, indigo energy for the $6^{th}$ chakra and brilliant energy for the $7^{th}$ chakra.

The whole process of cleansing and strengthening your own chakras should take about 30 min but it is an estimation. When you enter the energy world – you go into timelessness. The physical time has no authority over your consciousness when you are in timelessness.

If you meditate and still look at your watch, you are not in timelessness. Timelessness is when you just sense the vibrations of your own cells and do not notice the time. Physical time is the dimension where we created the illness. Timelessness is the healing dimension. Miracles occur in timelessness.

Chapter 8:

# HOW TO REMOVE THE ENERGY OF ILLNESS FROM YOUR ORGANS

> *Your hands can heal you ...You can remove the energy of illness from your body using your hands ...*

Our hands are the most sensitive body part to energy. Energy sensitivity spreads over the body in a predictable pattern. It starts with the hands, first the palms and then the backs of the hands, then the forearms, shoulders, forehead and then the rest of the body.

Healing with hands is based on the effect of bio-electromagnetism which has been proven by science. We are all part of a larger bioenergetic system that represent the whole human energy on the planet. We are interdependent upon one another for energy and for life. We share energy with each other continuously: give and receive. When we take steps to heal ourselves, we contribute positive energy to that big system that eventually can heal the world.

## HOW TO HEAL USING INTUITIVE HEALING

You can start by healing yourself: healing your aura, chakras, and organs.

To heal an organ, you can use two techniques. One technique is to work with the corresponding chakra. For example, for healing the heart – you can work with the heart chakra, for healing the liver – you can work with the solar plexus chakra, for healing the bladder – you can work with the sacral chakra … You can clean and strengthen the chakra.

Another technique is to work specifically with the organ. Working with organs includes:

- Removing the energy of illness from the organ … and then …
- Put positive energy in the organ.

Here are the principles of bio-electromagnetism for working with organs:

1. Each organ has specific energetic frequency. With practice, you can feel and differentiate it with your hands.
2. Each illness has a specific energetic frequency. This means, that if the organ is sick, it vibrates differently compare to the healthy organ. With practice, you can sense the vibrations with your hands.
3. It is possible to feel the sick energy and remove it from the organ using your hands.

## How to Remove the Energy of Illness from the Organ

1. Light a candle. Sit comfortably. Relax.
2. Bring your attention to the organ that you need to heal.
3. Take a few deep breaths. When exhaling, push the air through the organ that you need to heal, as if you are breathing through this organ.
4. Keep breathing through this organ until you feel, 'tingling and crawling' sensations in this organ - this is the subtle energy in this organ.
5. Now prepare your hands for a healing session. Bring your hands together and rub them until they are warm. Spread them apart 20-25 cm (10 inches) and feel as if you are holding an 'energy ball.' You should feel it as 'tingling and crawling' sensations in your hands. Tingling sensations mean that your hands are ready to sense energy.
6. Bring your right hand, if you are righthanded, next to the organ that you need to heal – about 20 cm from the organ. Find the edge of this organ aura. You feel it as resistance or tingling sensations in your hand.
7. Start anticlockwise movements with your hand. You feel it as if you are removing 'dust.' Throw this 'dust' into the candle and burn it. It is the energy of illness and must be burnt. To know the direction, put a watch on your body, face up. You will see which way is anticlockwise.
8. Keep cleansing the organ with anticlockwise movements until you feel lighter or do it for two minutes per organ.
After a sufficient cleansing, you can put positive energy into the organ. It is called strengthening of the organ.

## How to put positive energy into the organ.

1. Rub your hands together until they are warm. Spread your hands apart 20-25 cm. Feel that you are holding an 'energy ball.' You feel it as 'tingling and crawling' sensations in your hands.
2. Select a colour and visualise it as it enters the space between your hands. Now you are holding a red, orange, blue or a yellow ball of energy (read the explanations, how to choose a colour for different organs).
3. Bring this energy ball to the organ that you need to heal and start clockwise movements with your hands.
4. Visualise the energy of this colour is spreading through the organ. Feel tingling and crawling sensations in the organ.
5. Do clockwise movements with your hands for at least two minutes or until you feel that energy coming into this organ.

## How to Choose a Colour when Working with Organs

Colours are energetic frequencies perceived by the eye. Each energetic frequency affects the body differently. Therefore, it is possible to use the energy of colour to heal different problems.

There are energy rules on how to choose a colour when working with organs. In my book, "The Secret Energy of Your Body," I discuss this topic in greater details, but here let me give you a few tips.

1. Generally, when strengthening organs, you can choose the colour of the corresponding chakra. For example, for sexual organs – choose orange, for digestive organs – choose yellow, for organs in the head – choose indigo.
2. Each colour has energetic connections to the five senses - sight, smell, hearing, taste, and touch. I have researched these connections of forty-seven colours and found that each colour has a corresponding music, smell, food, plant/herb and a gemstone. With the help of your intuition you can feel these connections. If you are interested in the sensory alignment to develop your intuition, you can work with my, "Chromotherapy Healing Cards," which helps you connect to your five senses and balance them. http://dririnawebster.com/energy-healing-cards/ These healing cards are based on my personal research, "How to align 5 senses and be a whole person." Alignment of the five senses leads to the development of the sixth sense called intuition.
3. Be aware of the contraindications. Some colours are not compatible with certain illnesses. For example, you cannot use blue energy on a person with depression because depression vibrates blue. You need to stimulate a depressed person with a stimulating colour. Stimulating colours are red, orange, and yellow. Red is the best stimulator.

You cannot use red energy on a person who has anger problems because anger vibrates red. If a person has depression and anger problems at the same time, you cannot use red to stimulate him, but you can choose yellow or orange instead.

4. The universal healer is green, and it is generally a safe colour to use to speed up recovery and healing. The best purifier is white. The most detached colour is grey, and it is the best to use when you do energy reading on someone. To promote discipline, use black. To cool down use blue, to heat up use red.

## Energy Healing Rules

### Rule No. 1

Energy cleansing comes first. Always clean/remove energy from the organs first, before you put energy in the organs. If the organ is sick, it has a lot of toxic energy inside which must be removed. If you start putting energy in, without cleansing it first, the organ can become worse.

The same rule is applicable to chakras: Clean them first before you put energy in.

### Rule No. 2

Remember the directions of hands movements during a healing process:
- anticlockwise movements – energy out (cleansing)
- clockwise movements – energy in (strengthening).

Generally, our chakras rotate clockwise. Therefore, to remove energy you need to go anticlockwise, antivortex. To put energy in – clockwise.

Use a watch to understand the directions. Put a watch on the body face up to see the directions.

## Rule No. 3

During the healing, always burn the removed energy because it contains toxins. If you throw the toxic energy in the room, then somebody else picks it up or the energy comes back to you. Fire destroys everything, it is the best purifier. You should not use water to throw the toxic energy in, because water makes it a solution and the energy continues to circulate. Therefore, during healing sessions, you must burn it. I use normal white candles during my healing sessions. White colour is the greatest purifier.

## Rule No. 4

When you are working on healing yourself, eat energetically light foods. Look at the table below to see which foods are light and which are heavy:

| Fruits and vegetables | Light |
|---|---|
| Grains | Light |
| Nuts and seeds | Second lightest |
| Saltwater fish with scales | Third lightest |
| Fresh water fish | Third lightest |
| Seafood | Forth lightest |
| Fowl | Fifth lightest |
| Red meat | Heavy energy |
| Pork | Heavy energy |
| Eggs | Medium |
| Milk (cow, goat) | Medium (skim milk is light) |
| Butter and other fats | Heavy energy |
| Water | The lightest of all |

## Rule No. 5

During the time of healing, clean and energise your food before eating it. Food cleansing is performed by anticlockwise movements with your hands. Food energising is performed by clockwise movements with your hands. Read the chapter, 'How to Clean and Energise Your Food,' in this book.

# Chapter 9:
# WORKING WITH THE AURA

An aura is a biofield that surrounds humans and everything that is alive. The average human aura extends 1.5 m from the body, but the size varies depending on the person.

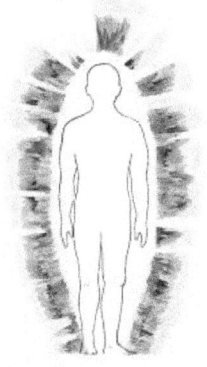 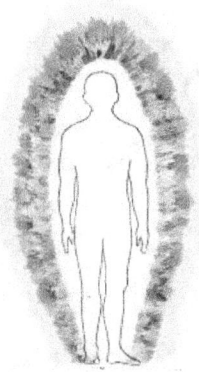 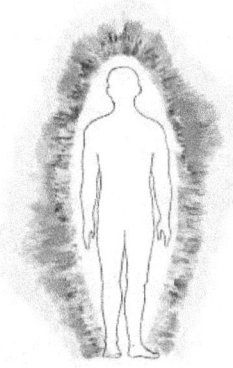

Sick aura due to low immunity, allergy or autoimmune illness.

Healthy aura: symmetrical and even.

Sick aura due to a psychotic illness or extreme stress.

On the global level, we were asked to respect the aura when social distancing rules were introduced. Social distancing rules (due to Covid-19) asked us to be at least 1.5 m away from each other. The size of the human aura is about 1.5 m. Therefore, Covid-19 taught us to respect our energy and be aware of it.

When people get sick their aura shrinks. You can see wasted aura in addicts or people who are in a state of hopelessness, such as cancer or severely depressed people etc.

The aura is the extension of chakras and has the same sequence of colours as chakras: red, orange, yellow, green, blue, indigo, and white (brilliant).

Also, in the aura of a person we can see the energy of other people. The more intimate the contact – the more of their energy is in us. We share our energy through emotions. Therefore, we should stay neutral, calm, and avoid getting emotionally involved in situations to protect our energy.

## For example:

> *Imagine you have problems at work with your boss. If your interactions with the person become emotional and you experience anger, frustrations, stress, anxiety, or resentment, you will be affected by the negative energy of this contact and eventually, you can develop an illness.*
>
> *If you learn to detach and be impersonal to personal situations, nothing can affect you. You will not take in the energy of the toxic person.*
>
> *The energy exchange occurs through emotions: How emotional you become during the contact.*
>
> *You cannot fake it. The calmness must be genuine.*

When you explore the aura, it is possible to sense the energy of the person's relationships, because of the energetic exchange.

People who keep their attention inside their body, have better and healthier auras.

People who are not aware of their own energy because their attention is always on other people, have weak and torn auras.

## The Colours of the Aura

A healthy person has all colours equally presented in their aura: red, orange, yellow, green, blue, indigo, and brilliant colours, the same sequence as chakras. Some people have more of a specific colour in their aura. This means that this chakra is dominant for them now. For example, if you see a lot of yellow around a person – it means that they are using their solar plexus now or it is their dominant chakra in general. If someone has a lot of blue around them – it means they are using their throat chakra a lot. If a person has a distinctive red energy around him – he relies on the tribal power a lot, maybe at the expense of the other chakras.

Aura colours change depending on the state of health, age, emotions, diets, and behaviours.

## How to See Auras

Seeing an aura is easy. You need to use your peripheral vison to see the aura. You cannot see it with direct vision.

Practice it with a friend by having them stand in front of a white or neutral-coloured wall. Then, focus on their forehead, somewhere between their eyes. Keep looking at them gently, without straining your eyes until your peripheral vision starts showing different colours. Do not move your eyes, keep looking at their forehead and use your peripheral vision to see their aura. Initially you see fine colours but with practice you can see brighter colours around the person.

Another way to see the aura is to do it with yourself using a mirror. You need to stand in front of a white or a neutral-coloured wall. Take a mirror and look at your own forehead, somewhere between your eyes. Keep looking gently, without straining your eyes until your peripheral vision starts showing different colours. Do not move your eyes, because direct vision will not help you see the aura. Use your peripheral vision.

## How to scan Aura on yourself?

1. Sit on a chair or lie down and relax.
2. Put your hands about 25 cm (10 inches) from your own head and try to find the edge of your aura. If you do not feel the edge, bring your hands a few inches closer until you find it.

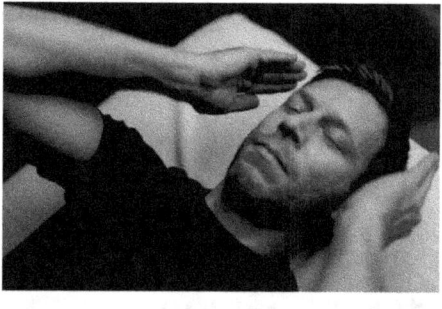

3. When you feel the edge of your aura you should start sensing 'tingling or crawling' sensations in your hands. You may also feel warmth or other sensations in your hands.
4. Move your hands down and explore your throat, chest, belly, pelvis, hips, legs, and feet. Follow along the edge of your aura. Feel the edge as tingling and crawling sensations in your hands.

5. Notice how the energy feels different in different body parts. The key here is to sense the subtle energy layer by layer, as you scan your aura.

**NOTE!** When you scan yourself, it is important to not just feel it with your hands, but also feel it with your body. For example, if you scan your head, you feel 'tingling and crawling' sensations in your hands and, also, feel it in your head (your temples, cheeks, forehead, nose, lips and etc.) Your body should sense your hands movements without touching it.

## How to Scan the Aura on another Person

1. A person can sit on a chair or lie down and relax.
2. You put your hands about 25 cm (10 inches) from the person's head and try to find the edge of his/her aura. If you do not feel the edge, bring your hands a bit closer until you find it.
3. When you feel the edge you start sensing tingling or crawling sensations in your hands. You may also feel it as warmth.
4. Move your hands down the person's body and explore his/her neck, shoulders, back, hips, legs, feet, and toes. Follow the edge of the aura.
5. Notice how the energy feels different in different body parts. Acknowledge the quality of the person's aura: density, temperature, colour, consistency etc.

## Basic diagnostic principles when sensing the aura.

### Principle 1:

The first tip to remember when sensing an aura is that a healthy person vibrates, **'cool mind – fire in the belly.'** The Aura should be cool around the head and warm around the belly. All variations from this rule are abnormalities and imply problems. 'Cool mind' means that the person is present, focused and calm. 'Fire in the belly' means – the person has enough physical energy to act on what his mind has conceived and can materialise his dreams into reality. People who overthink and spend hours listening to brain chatter, have warm energy around their head and cool energies around their belly. They waste a lot of energy from the head, overthinking, that depletes their belly. They do not have enough energy to act on their intentions. They have difficulties materialising their dreams.

Also remember, that at the top of the body, chakras are cool colours: blue, indigo, and white. At the bottom of the body chakras are warm: red, orange, and yellow. This is another reason why we feel, 'cool mind – fire in the belly,' on a healthy person.

### Principle 2:

If the aura is **bigger at the front of a person and smaller at the back** – it means the person projects himself/herself to the future: worries about the future and having anxiety. Anxiety is associated with worrying about 'what the future brings.'

## Principle 3:

If the aura is **bigger at the back of a person and smaller at the front** – it means the person projects himself/herself into the past: regrets the past, holds on to the past, blames other people from the past. It also means a depression state. Depression is associated with holding on to the past and the inability to move on.

## Principle 4:

If the aura is **bigger on the left side and smaller on the right side** – it means the person has too much feminine energy and not enough masculine energy. They become too emotional, too sensual, but have no physical power or capacity to 'go for it.'

## Principle 5:

If the aura is **bigger on the right side and smaller on the left side** – it means the person has too much masculine energy and not enough feminine energy. They are always on the go, overdoing things, behaving like a macho but denying their emotions.

## Principle 6:

If the aura is **bigger at the top and smaller at the feet** – it means the person is too spiritual, maybe even too 'airy-fairy,' and is disconnected from the physical side of life.

## Principle 7:

If the aura is **bigger at the bottom and smaller at the top** – it means the person is too materialistic and only cares about the physical side of life such as bills, house and food, but is disconnected from the spiritual life and the higher purpose.

> **NOTE!**
>
> **A healthy aura looks symmetrical, even, consistent, equal density all around the body.** All variations from that imply problems.

## How to Clean the Aura

We pick up energy from other people and environments. It is possible to clean the aura and remove all toxins and blockages from it.

## How to Clean your Own Aura

There are two consecutive steps to clean your aura: General sweeping and Local sweeping.

## Step 1: General sweeping (from top to bottom)

1. Find the edge of your own aura.
2. Start sweeping motions with your hands from the top of your head down to your feet. Follow the edge of your aura.
3. When you sweep, collect the negative energy with your hands and throw it in the fire (a candle) and burn the toxic energy.
4. Do sweeping motions until you feel lighter.

## Step 2: Local sweeping (local areas only)

1. During general sweeping identify areas in your aura that vibrate abnormally: denser or depleted.
2. Sweep these areas individually. For example, if during general sweeping you identified that your right shoulder vibrates abnormally, then do sweeping just around the right shoulder. This is local sweeping.
Or if you feel that your throat vibrates abnormally, then do local sweeping just around the throat area.
3. Throw the negative energy into the fire (a candle) and burn the toxins.

> **General sweeping – you sweep the aura from head to toes.**
>
> **Local sweeping – you sweep only local areas.**

If you need to clean the aura on another person – use the same techniques: General sweeping and Local sweeping. Always burn the removed energy.

### How to Clean the Aura on another Person

1. Have the person sit on a chair, so you can walk around them and clean their aura from all sides. Ask the person to relax and close his/her eyes.
2. With your hands, find the edge of their aura.
3. Start sweeping motions with your hands and sweep their aura from head to toes. Do sweeping from all sides of their body.
4. As you sweep, throw the removed energy into the candle, and burn the toxins.

5. When you sweep from head to toes, identify areas that vibrate abnormally: denser areas or depleted areas.
6. Do local sweeping of these areas. Burn the toxins.

## How to Re-Create the Aura

After a sufficient cleansing, you can re-create the aura. Aura re-creation means restoring all the colours in the aura and making it strong again. You can do it on yourself and you can do it on another person. Aura re-creation promotes health and wellbeing.

## How to Re-Create your own Aura

1. Sit in a comfortable position and clean your aura first (read how to clean your aura).
   Then, bring your attention to your 1st chakra and visualise a red ball of energy rotating at the base of your spine.
   - Feel the red energy there, then spread it throughout your body and then bring red energy outside of your body.
   - Surround yourself with red energy. This is the 1st layer of your aura – the red.
   - Bring your hands 10-15 cm (4 inches) from your body and feel the red layer around your body. Feel red vibrations.
2. Bring your attention to your 2nd chakra (pelvis) and visualise an orange ball of energy rotating there.
   - Feel orange vibrations inside your pelvis, then spread them throughout your body and then bring them outside of your body.

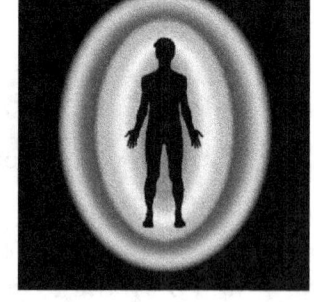

- Surround yourself with orange energy – this is the 2$^{nd}$ layer of your aura.
- Bring your hands 15-20 cm (7 inches) from your body and feel the orange layer of energy around you.
3. Bring your attention to your 3$^{rd}$ chakra, upper belly, and visualise yellow ball of energy rotating there.
- Feel yellow vibrations inside your belly, then spread them throughout your body and then bring yellow energy outside of your body.
- Surround yourself with yellow – this is the 3$^{rd}$ layer of your aura.
  Bring your hands 20-30 cm (11 inches) from your body and feel this yellow layer around you.
4. Bring your attention to your 4$^{th}$ chakra, chest, and visualise green ball of energy rotating there.
- Feel green vibrations inside your chest, then spread them throughout the body and then bring green energy outside of your body.
- Surround yourself with green energy – this is the 4$^{th}$ layer of your aura.
- Bring your hands 30-40 cm (15 inches) from your body and feel this green layer around you.
5. Bring your attention to your 5$^{th}$ chakra, throat, and visualise a blue ball of energy rotating there.
- Feel blue vibrations inside your throat, then spread them throughout your body and then bring blue energy outside of your body.
- Surround yourself with blue energy – this is the 5$^{th}$ layer of your aura.

## HOW TO HEAL USING INTUITIVE HEALING

- Bring your hands 40-50 cm (19 inches) from your body and feel this blue layer around you.
6. Bring your attention to your 6th chakra, forehead, and visualise an indigo ball of energy rotating there.
- Feel indigo vibrations inside your head, then spread them throughout your body and then bring indigo outside of your body.
- Surround yourself with indigo energy – this is the 6th layer of your aura.
- Bring your hands 50-60 cm (21 inches) from your body and feel this indigo layer around you.
7. Bring your attention to your 7th chakra, the top of your head, and visualise a brilliant ball of energy rotating there.
- Feel brilliant vibrations at the top of your head, then spread them throughout the body and then bring them outside of your body.
- Surround yourself with the brilliant energy – this is the 7th layer of your aura – the energy of Divine connection.
- Bring your hands 60 -80 cm (30 inches) from your body and feel this brilliant layer around you.

Now you have re-created all seven layers of your aura.

To finish the process of aura re-creation, put a cover of protection around your aura. Visualise that there is a golden shell around your aura, and you are sitting in a gold colour egg. Gold colour repels negativity. Say a protective mantra: **"Stabilise, stabilise, stabilise ... protect, protect, protect."**

## How to Re-Create the Aura on another Person

The steps to do it on another person are the same. First, tell the person that you will guide them to re-create their aura. They must participate in the process and feel their own energy. The effectiveness of aura re-creation depends on how much the person feels their own energy during the process. Their internal awareness is the key.

Here are the steps to follow:
1. Sit the person on a chair, so you can feel their aura from all sides.
- Ask the person to focus on his/her $1^{st}$ chakra and visualise red ball of energy at the base of their spine. Ask them to feel red vibrations inside.
- With your hands sense the energy of their $1^{st}$ chakra. When you do that, you direct their attention to this chakra.
- Ask the person to feel the red energy at the base of their spine, then ask them to spread the red energy throughout their body and then bring it outside of their body. They should feel it - the power of the red energy inside and around them.
- With your hands, sense the red energy around their body - this is the $1^{st}$ layer of their aura - tribal energy.
2. Ask the person to focus on their $2^{nd}$ chakra and visualise the orange ball of energy rotating inside their pelvis.
- With your hands sense the energy of their $2^{nd}$ chakra. When you do that, you direct their attention to this chakra.
- Ask them to feel orange vibrations in their pelvis, then ask them to spread the orange energy throughout their body

and then bring it outside of their body. This is the 2nd layer of their aura – the orange layer.
3. Do the same steps for the 3rd, 4th, 5th, 6th, and 7th chakras. For the 3rd layer – ask them to feel yellow energy, for the 4th layer ask them to feel green energy, for the 5th layer – blue energy, for the 6th layer – indigo energy and for 7th layer – brilliant energy.
4. To finish the process of aura re-creation on another person, put gold colour energy around their aura and ask them to visualise that they are sitting in a gold coloured egg. Say a protective mantra, **"Stabilise, stabilise, stabilise ... protect, protect, protect."**

## Chapter 10:
# BODY SHAPES

People have different body shapes. By looking at a body shape of a person, you can tell his or her story. Our body protects itself by growing fat around the body parts. Fat is protection. Fat distribution is connected to the emotional issues from which a person needs protection. This process is unconscious and is connected to the chakras.

Here is the guide:

> **Unproportionally fat legs** - means anger at a father and/or other family conflicts. Their body is protecting the 1$^{st}$ chakra area.
>
> **Unproportionally fat bottom and hips** - means controlling relationships. The person's relationship style is controlling. Engagement in power games, co-dependency, and tug of war situations. Feeling defensive or being, 'needy,' in relationships. Their body is protecting the 2$^{nd}$ chakra organs.
>
> **Unproportionally fat waist** – low self-esteem. Taking responsibility for others but losing their own self-esteem and identity. Pushover. Constant need for the approval of others. People pleasing. Dislike of the self. Having intuitions about other people but not about themself. Their body is protecting the 3$^{rd}$ chakra organs.

> **Unproportionally big breasts** – problems with nurturing. Trying to nurture others more than she nurtures herself. She is a person who calls everybody around, "darling," but she is crying inside for self-love. In fact, she does not even know what self-love is. Her body is protecting the 4$^{th}$ chakra organs.
>
> **Unproportionally fat neck** – hiding family secrets about the unspoken things. Past hurts, regrets, blame about family situations that should be spoken about, but they cannot because of the shame and guilt. For example, a person who was sexually abused by a family member and was forbidden to talk about it because of the shame she or he would bring to their family – can develop unproportionally fat neck as a result. Their body is protecting the 5$^{th}$ chakra organs. This is relevant to any kind of abuse that they were forbidden to speak about.

As you see, fat grows in the body according to the disfunctions in the chakras. Some people have a mix of problems. You can still evaluate them using this guide. Knowing these rules helps to understand people better. This guide is quite accurate.

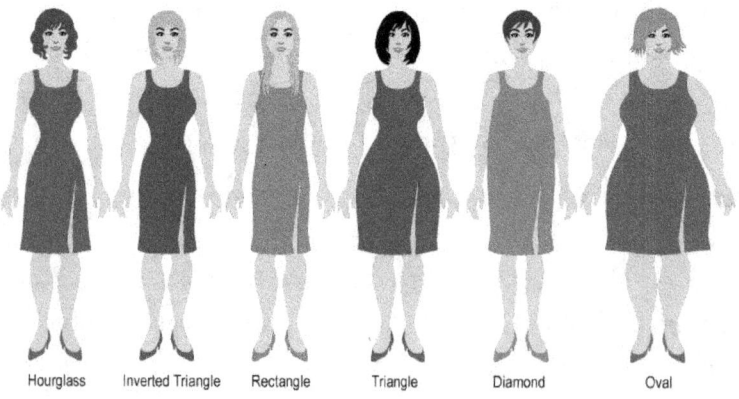

Hourglass · Inverted Triangle · Rectangle · Triangle · Diamond · Oval

## Chapter 11:
# HOW TO DIFFERENTIATE INTUITION FROM FEAR, BRAIN CHATTER, AND OTHER FALSE PERCEPTIONS

When working with intuition, it is important to differentiate genuine intuitive voices from the voices of fear and brain chatter.

Intuition is a very delicate voice which is committed to our well-being. Intuition is our best friend and advisor. You experience intuition as a gut feeling, a hunch, a physical sensation, or a dream. It is a subtle voice, neutral, non-emotional but has a deep sense of inner knowing. It may bring a negative news but in a subtle way. Intuition is always about the present moment: how to act here and now. Intuition is not about past fears or future anxieties.

Brain chatter is loud, continuous, domineering, and annoying. The content is based on your previous experiences or your fantasies about the future. It takes you away from the present moment and it is difficult to stop. The content of the brain chatter is very repetitive and useless. It does not support your wellbeing.

Fear has cruel, demeaning, or delusional content. It makes you feel emotional. It brings chaos and you feel that you do not know what to do. Fear always has a charge, negative or positive. A positive charge is when you think about something, "Oh my God, it's so good!!!" But later it appears to be not so good. You just had a positive charge that came from fear, but you mistook it for intuitions.

Intuition has no charge. It is not driven by any positive or negative expectations. It comes from the centre of your body and feels like inner knowing. The intuitive perceptions are crystal clear but not emotional, (rather detached). You feel as if you are watching a movie. Intuition has a compassionate, affirming tone and gives clarity on what to do now, in the present moment.

**NOTE**: If you get impressions about people or situations and you feel emotional or judgemental about the impressions, consider these impressions as emotionally contaminated. Wait until you start receiving neutral or detached sensations. These neutral sensations are more likely to be genuine intuitions.

To summarise the differences between intuition, fear, and brain chatter, look at the table below.

| Intuition | Fear | Brain Chatter |
|---|---|---|
| Has a compassionate, supportive feel. | Has a strong emotional charge. It screams at you. | Has charge: Positive or negative. Always judging and comparing. Always thinking, "black or white." |
| Brings clarity about what to do right now. Always based on the present time. | The information is based on previous experiences and touches the past wounds. | The information is based on the past experiences or future expectations. Not in the now. |
| Provides clear perceptions that are, 'seen' first, then felt. | Brings chaos. Reduces centeredness and confidence. | Separates you from the present moment. Takes you to the other place. |
| Brings a detached sensation, as if you are watching a movie. | Makes you feel emotional: scared or stressed. Chaotic. You do not know what to do. | Brings many thoughts and emotions – all at the same time. You feel overwhelmed. Scattered. |
| The voice is subtle, gentle, quiet, comes in a flash. Comes from the middle part of your body. | The voice is loud, it screams at you. The voice is constant and is difficult to stop. Comes from the head. | The voice is continuous, loud, and overbearing. Difficult to stop. Comes from the head. |

## How to Protect yourself from Fear and Brain Chatter?

### Here are the steps to follow:
1. Focus on your breathing. When anxious, people tend to hold their breath. But to protect your energy you should do the opposite: Breathe deeply and consciously.
2. Shielding technique: visualise a golden shield around your body which protects your energy and repels negativity.
3. Meditate daily. Sensing subtle body energy is the best meditation to connect to your body and organs. It helps to strengthen your own energy and makes you become neutral to the energy of others.
4. Set your limits with others. Be able to say "no" with calm but determined tone of voice.
5. Use water to remove the negative energy from your body. Wash your face, wash your hands, or have a shower and visualise the negative energy being washed away.
6. Burn a white candle for purification of space. You can also burn sage.
7. Stop thinking about the negative people and negative energy. By thinking about them you give them more power.
8. If possible, break contact with an energy vampire to stop the transfer of toxins.
9. Do aura cleansing techniques on yourself: General sweeping technique and local sweeping technique (read the chapter, 'How to Clean the Aura').
10. Do chakra's cleansing on yourself with anticlockwise movements of your hands. (read the chapter 'How to do Chakra Cleansing').

**NOTE!** I found that if you overemphasise protection, your body will start to feel that it needs protection at all times, that it is not safe. Therefore, the best protection is practicing detachment and impersonal mind. In this case you do not even need any protection. You can be with people at any time, but you are not affected by their energy.

## Two Powerful Exercises to Stop Brain Chatter

1. The Blackboard and the Sponge exercise.

Sit in a comfortable chair, close your eyes, and imagine that you have a blackboard on the inside of your forehead. Also imagine that you have an eraser in your hand. Once you have visualised this, your job is to look at the blackboard, and keep it black. When a thought appears on the blackboard, move your imaginary hand, and wipe it clean.

I did this exercise for 10 minutes every day before I went to bed. At first my hand with the eraser was moving very fast, but, over time, I learned to keep the blackboard clean. When I managed that, I noticed that my brain became still and calm. Brain chatter went away.

2. Feeling your body, observing the sensations in your body.

The exercise consists of observing the physical sensations in your body, noticing the differences between one side of your body and the other side, such as how your left hand might feel differently compare to your right hand, how the right side of your neck may be more tense than the left side, how one part of your body may be warmer, more numb, less tingly, harder to feel etc.

The exercise should be done regularly, starting from your palms, then moving to the entire hands, the wrists, lower arms, elbow joints, upper arms, shoulders, the neck, scalp, the top of the head, the face, jaw, eyes and then down to the throat, chest, breasts, the diaphragm, upper belly, lower belly, pelvis, hips, upper legs, knees, the lower legs, ankles, feet and finally your toes ... The key is to observe without judgment. This is similar to the body scan meditation.

Practicing these two techniques regularly will help you stop your brain chatter and help you hear your intuition calmly and clearly.

# Chapter 12:
# HOW TO STOP FEAR – THE INTERNAL SMILE

The Internal Smile is a powerful practice of healing, which has been practised in ancient China. The wise men have achieved great health, happiness and longevity using ... the Internal Smile.

In Taoism, negative emotions are regarded as low-quality energy. Many people spend their lives in anger, sadness, depression, fear, anxiety, and other kinds of stressful energy. These energies cause chronic illness and drain our vitality.

The Internal Smile is a sincere smile from the whole body: including all organs, glands, muscles, bones, and nervous system. It produces high-quality energy that can heal, and eventually transform itself into even higher quality energy.

A sincere smile sends the energy of love that has power to heal and transform. Just remember the time when you were upset or physically ill, and someone, perhaps even a stranger, smiled sincerely, and suddenly, you felt better.

In Ancient China, wise men discovered the power of the Inner Smile. They practiced the Internal Smile on themselves. They used their own subtle energy and formed higher vibration energy, which created health, happiness, and longevity in the body.

The Internal Smile is like a delight in love or a pleasure of love, and love can restore and rejuvenate.

The Internal Smile directs loving energy into our organs and glands, which is necessary for healing and good life.

The Internal Smile is the best for neutralising any kind of stress.

**There are Eleven Steps to Practicing the Inner Smile**

1. Sit comfortably and keep your spine in an upright position. Relax …
2. Take a few deep, slow breaths, noticing how your abdomen rises and relaxes with each breath. Empty your mind and let go of thoughts.
3. Rest the tip of your tongue gently on the roof of your mouth.
4. Smile gently, allowing your lips to feel full and smooth as they spread to the side and lift just slightly. This smile should be like the Mona Lisa smile.

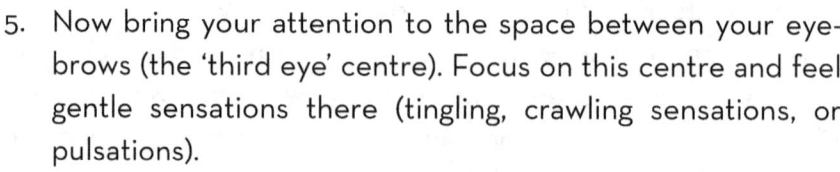

5. Now bring your attention to the space between your eyebrows (the 'third eye' centre). Focus on this centre and feel gentle sensations there (tingling, crawling sensations, or pulsations).
6. Bring your attention now to the middle of your head, (the centre of your brain). This place is called the Crystal Palace in Taoism – home to the pineal, pituitary, thalamus, and

hypothalamus glands. Feel the energy gathering in the middle of your head.
7. Allow this energy to flow forward into your eyes. Feel your eyes becoming 'smiling eyes.' To enhance this, you can imagine that you're gazing into the eyes of the person who you love the most, and they're gazing back at you ... infusing your eyes with this quality of loving-kindness and delight.
8. Now, direct the energy of your smiling eyes back and down into some place in your body where you need healing. It might be a place where you have recently had an injury or illness. In any case, smile down into that place within your body, and feel that the place is opening to receive the smile-energy.
9. Continue to smile into that place within your body and let it absorb this smile-energy like a sponge soaks up water.
10. When this feels complete, direct your inner attention, with its smile-energy, into your solar plexus, and feel warmth and brightness in your belly now.
11. Release the tip of your tongue from the roof of your mouth and release the smile. Feel the smile-energy spreading through the rest of your body.

When your energy grows, you will have more energy to work on your talents and skills. You will become more flexible and adaptable. You will know what you want in life and how to achieve this. You will start to heal ...

## Chakras and the Effect of the Internal Smile

All chakras are affected by the Internal smile healing, but the most significant changes occur in the 4th chakra, (heart chakra) and the 1ˢᵗ chakra, (tribal). The Internal smile healing restores your sense on home – or what 'home' means to you. When I say 'home' – I mean, 'your own temple' – your own body - the only temple you have for the rest of your life.

Look at the table below and see how each chakra is affected by the Internal smile healing.

| Chakra | How it is Affected by the Internal Smile Healing |
|---|---|
| 1 Chakra - Tribal Power | Makes you feel safe, secure, supported, and protected in your own body. |
| 2 Chakra - Relationships | Helps you attract better partners because you feel safe and secure in yourself. |
| 3 Chakra - Solar Plexus | Helps you improve your self-esteem and feel good about yourself. |
| 4 Chakra - Heart Chakra | Supports unconditional love. Makes your heart thrive and blossom with love. |
| 5 Chakra - Throat | Helps you communicate lovingly and express yourself clearly and with love. |
| 6 Chakra – Third Eye | Helps you see others with love. |
| 7 Chakra – Divine Connection | Helps you feel oneness with the Divine. |

# Chapter 13:
# INTUITIVE HEALING FOR RELATIONSHIPS

Our relationships influence our health and longevity. I believe that all relationships need intuitive healing, even the good ones. Intuitive healing helps to understand yourself better and how you react to people. Therefore, we need intuitive healing to have happy relationships.

I read somewhere that the spiritual reason why we have relationships is to understand ourselves. I believe this is true.

If you look at your partners, you will see your mirror image. Before you attract him/her, you open a door for them to come in.

It sounds strange but many people do not see their contribution in the development of their relationships. They consider their relationships as a fluke, or accidents which just happened to them. This is counterintuitive.

The fact is that relationships are our reflections. Looking at our partners we see who we are – spiritually, emotionally, intuitively.

Very often we are not willing to look at ourselves through a loved one. But relationships, whether you like it or not, follow certain rules, aligned with our chakras and the chakras of our partners.

You should know these energetic rules according to which we develop relationships.

## Rule 1: Complementation

Partners are meant to serve one another, and their relationships are interdependent. During our life we are trying to achieve our highest potential, but what is stopping us is the masks, or subpersonalities that we develop to survive. From a young age we learn to adjust to our parents, school, society, and other people by behaving differently in each situation. Each behaviour becomes a mask. In relationships, our masks interact. The power of attraction is based on the principle of complementation. For example, a victim will always attract a vampire; a damsel will get a knight who'll initially save her but then, "lock her in a castle"; a mother will always attract a child; a servant needs a master and the like.

## Rule 2: The Shadow Reveals

In relationships, a man helps a woman to understand her subpersonality that is hidden from her own awareness – her shadow. A male's behaviour in a relationship reveals those sub-personalities that women suppress:

For example:
- If a man drinks, then a woman does not realise that she supresses him. His drinking means: I must be unconscious for you to care of me.
- If a man abuses a woman, means that she is stuck in a victim mode. His behaviour means: I must be dangerous to you, so you have somebody to fear.

- If a man becomes idle when a woman takes all the responsibilities and becomes like a mother to him - his behaviour is saying - I should be a child for you to teach me and look after me.
- If a man is cheating with other women, it means he could not make his 'first woman' happy — his mother. His behaviour is saying: I must be a traitor for you to stop being a victim, (referring to his mother but living with his wife).

In relationships, a woman helps a man to see what he has already achieved. In doing so, it does not matter if he has achieved high or low.

- When a man is strong and confident, a woman complements him with her softness and trust.
- When a man is helpless, beside him is an omnipotent woman.
- When he is needy, beside him is a significant woman.
- When he is a sufferer, she is a counsellor.
- When he is a liar, she is a truth revealer.

## Rule 3: Parental Influence

A man always aims to satisfy the needs of two women: A wife, and a mother. When one of them drags his attention, it evokes protest in the other.

A woman wants from her man what her father could not give her. Based on security needs, she always projects her negative past experiences with previous men, onto her current relationship. A father is her first man and emotional patterns of their relationship affect all her future relationships. Intuitive healing is needed to understand and change this programming.

## Rule 4: Evolution of Roles

A husband and a father have different functions. A father must protect and provide for his daughter. A husband wants to protect and provide for his wife only when she inspires him.

Then happiness of a woman is not in her man. She is her own happiness. Happiness of any individual cannot be outside of their own body. If you wait for happiness to come from your partner, this means you are making this person responsible (guilty) for the absence of your own happiness. Happiness in a relationship comes from understanding the conflict of sub-personalities and their roles in a relationship. If at least one person refuses to play their role, the conflict will be solved because it is based on co-dependency. For example, if a child starts taking his own responsibility, there is no need for a mother to be overbearing; if a princess starts doing for herself what she is expecting the knight to do for her – there is no need for a knight to, 'lock her in the castle.'

Most shadow sub-personalities that destroy relationships are parental messages. By realising that you are playing a role, you can remove this mask and become free.

## Rule 5: Your Partner's Behaviour is your Feedback

Your partner's behaviour is your own feedback, through which you can see your own subpersonalities. Looking at a man's bad behaviour, a woman must realise what is there inside her that is stopping her from feeling loved and cherished.

Looking at a woman's behaviour, a man must realise to which extend he is in harmony with the world.

## How to Differentiate Intuition from Fear in Relationships

We have all heard the phrase, "You feel it – when you meet your man." And the same is true in the opposite case: Your body feels when the person is not your person.

Neuroscientific studies show that our body knows when we need to stay away from a person, even before our mind understands it. And here is how:

1. You feel tension in the body, even if the person looks very kind. You know there is no reason to be nervous, but you just cannot relax being with this person.
2. You do not understand his/her body language. Maybe his/her eyes seem empty or his smile is insincere. Maybe you feel that his body language is aggressive, although he talks very nicely. This discrepancy confuses you.

    Our subconscious mind notices small nuances in the energy of another person. So, if you feel something is wrong, listen to your intuition.
3. Sometimes you feel that he has a secret that you would not like. This is important to acknowledge, because a person who is honest with you, would not cause any suspicions.
4. You do not like his smell. It is not about his perfume. It is about a natural smell. There are such things as pheromones, and they affect attractiveness and compatibility.
5. Even when you are happy with him, you do not feel like everything is as it should be. You cannot logically explain it, but you keep feeling that something is wrong.

6. You observe him, but not in a good way. It is like you're afraid of him, and every second you try to guess his true intentions. You, subconsciously, feel like you are watching a predator, just like a deer looking at the hunter, waiting for his next move.
7. When you first met, you felt a physical rejection, but you just tried to be nice. The truth is that your body was right. You should trust your intuition.
8. You do not feel physical attraction to him. Your body does not connect to his body. Without this attraction, relationships will not survive for very long. You may become, 'just friends,' but not intimate partners.

If you ignore these intuitive signs and still go into a relationship, you are likely to develop health problems, or the relationship will end leaving you disappointed. You should always respect your body signals, even if the logic mind thinks different.

## How to Heal Relationships

- To heal your relationships, first, you need to realise **what role** you play in relationships and become aware of your behavioural pattern that you use to attract a partner
- Secondly, if you are in a relationship and want to continue this relationship, you can use energy healing techniques to clean the energy of your partner and your own energy.

- You can clean their aura regularly, especially before having intimate contact. You can also clean their chakras and organs. See how to do that in the previous chapters in this book.
- You should clean your own energy regularly, especially before and after having intimate contacts.
- Use your intuition to know how much and how often you should clean their energy. Be sensitive to their feelings and always explain to them what you are doing. Never do anything harmful or against their will. All energy healing techniques should be performed using mutual agreement.

If your partner is against using these techniques on him/her, ask why they feel negative about energy healing. It could be because you and your partner are not spiritually compatible. Spiritual compatibility is important for having good relationships.

## Chakras and Relationships

All chakras are involved and affected by your relationships, but the most significant changes occur in the 2nd chakra (relationships) and the 4th chakra (heart chakra). When you heal your relationships, you create changes in your chakras and the chakras of your partner.

Look at the table below and see how each chakra is affected by relationship healing.

| Chakra | How it is Affected by Relationship Healing |
|---|---|
| 1 Chakra - Tribal Power | Healing your relationships helps you see the past programming that you got from your family and heal it. |
| 2 Chakra - Relationships | Helps to understand the role you play when attracting relationships. It is the mask you put on when in relationships. If you understand the mask – you can change it. |
| 3 Chakra - Solar Plexus | Relationship healing improves your self-esteem. |
| 4 Chakra - Heart Chakra | It helps you experience unconditional love in relationships. |
| 5 Chakra - Throat | It helps you speak your truth, (your true needs, wants and desires) in relationships. |
| 6 Chakra - Third Eye | It helps you see the truth about your relationships and differentiate the truth from illusions. |
| 7 Chakra - Divine Connection | It helps you realise the Divinity of your relationships. |

# Chapter 14:
# INTUITIVE HEALING FOR PARENTS

Intuitive healing is something that all parents must practice. Working as a paediatrician in Russia for many years made me realise that our feelings of being hurt in the past, are connected to our children's illnesses today.

Therefore, if your child has problems ... think ... maybe by looking into your own unhealed wounds, you will find some answers ...

Look at this interesting story ...

> A mother of a two-year old boy has recently told me that her son has been diagnosed with deafness. It was a second child in the family, and he was not particularly welcome. The family really wanted a girl, not a boy. When she had an ultrasound to find out the baby's sex and the doctor said, "You have a boy," her husband said loudly, "Well ... nothing we can do to change it ..."
>
> Whether he was unhappy with the news of her second pregnancy, or if something else in the marriage was making him unhappy – we do not know.

But the woman's feelings of being wronged by her husband affected her feelings towards her son. She felt dubious: from one side, she loved her son but on the other side, she felt resentment towards the boy – the feelings she tried to deny and was uncomfortable to admit.

The wound caused by the words of her husband stopped her from unconditionally loving and accepting her child.

The family went through a lot of conflicts, tears, mixed feelings about the child's illness. They blamed each other and argued about what might have caused the child's illness, and whose side of the family it came from.

In general, this reaction to a shock was quite justified.

A surprise came later ...

After the boy got a hearing aid and started to hear voices and sounds, I met the woman again. She was a new person ... She told me, that when she witnessed her child's first reaction to her voice, she experienced a miracle transformation.

When her son heard her voice for the very first time, he started to smile, laugh, and then opened his arms to embrace her with joy and innocence ...

**"This is what real LOVE is ..."** – the words that came to her at that moment. From this moment, she realised how insignificant her grudges, hurts and past wounds were. She went through a stage of forgiveness of her husband, and the family reunited with Love and Faith.

Now, listen to this carefully ...

It is the child's illness that allowed the parents to forgive each other and come together again; to heal their child. Their son's illness became the reason for family to grow stronger and love each other again.

What I am suggesting is that the child's illness was a message to his parents to learn to love unconditionally. Love each other and love life in general.

> **NOTE - IMPORTANT:**
>
> To heal a child, first you need to look at your own emotions and release all hurts, grudges, victimhood, criticism, blame and the feelings of being stuck. Then from this pure state of forgiveness, you should act and do the necessary steps towards healing and recovery.

**Health problems in infants are connected to the problems in the heads and hearts of their parents.** The problems which started at the time of conception, during pregnancy and after the birth of the child.

If your child is sick, look at what you need to change in your life, what you need to release and get rid of completely. Then find new things that you need to establish instead.

And lastly, Love is here to help you ... No matter how tough, unfair or hurtful your circumstances are; still find Love. Send love to the person who hurt you or has been unfair to you. What they did was the only thing they could do at the time. It was the only thing they were aware of.

Forgive them unconditionally and release all the negative energy that is holding you back. And of course, thank the father (mother) of your child. At least for the fact, that now, you have this miracle – your child. Send them love every day because this Love goes not just to them but your child as well.

## Heal Your Own Inner Child First

If you do not heal your own childhood problems, you will repeat the same mistakes with your own children. You will do it unconsciously, just because your own inner child is not safe.

The inner child is the part in your psyche that contains innocence, creativity, awe, and wonder. When you are connected to your inner child, you feel excited, energised, and inspired by life. When you are disconnected, you feel bored, unhappy, and empty. Your inner child lives in the 1$^{st}$ chakra and originate from your family.

If your childhood was problematic, then your inner child becomes, 'wounded,' or 'abandoned.'

The abandoned inner child feels unaccepted, undervalued, and misunderstood. It does not feel like it belongs and suffers from loneliness, isolation, and rejection. It feels that there is no place to call 'home.' It seeks constant approval, and experiences confusion and self-doubt. It has difficulty with relating to people because it cannot feel like it belongs.

The wounded inner child feels that he/she is wounded, neglected, and mistreated. It continuously re-experiences the feelings of trauma and being violated. The wounded child sees the world like an unsafe place and feels that there is nobody to trust. Therefore, it turns to blame, criticism and often has dysfunctional relationships with others and with himself.

## How to Heal Your Inner Child

To heal your own inner child, you need to connect to it and listen to its needs and desires. Then, you need to love it, nurture it, and play with it. A child wants to play and feel loved.

There are a few ways to connect and play with your inner child.

## Method 1:

### Listen to your inner child's needs and wants

Take a pen and a paper and answer the following questions:
- My favourite childhood toy was ...
- My favourite childhood game was ...
- My favourite movies are ...
- My favourite activities when I was a youth were ...
- My favourite songs are ...
- My favourite books are ...
- My favourite way to dress is ...
- What characters I would like to dress up as to feel good about myself, (to express how I am, my creativity and my desires). For example: A gypsy, a princess, a pirate, a national costume etc ...

Look for a common theme that emerges when answering these questions. The theme is a clue to what you should be doing to enjoy your life. This will help you to connect to your inner child, recover your sense of power and feel good about yourself as a parent.

## Method 2:

### Connect to Yourself as a Newborn

Find a photo of yourself as a newborn. If you do not have a newborn photo, you can use a photo of yourself as a small child. Look at this photo ... Close your eyes and imagine holding yourself as a baby in your arms. Feel the energy of the baby. Hold and hug the baby. Acknowledge your feelings. Do you feel loving and nurturing or cold and distant? Ask how you, as a baby, feel about your life? Are you happy and joyful? Or scared and stressed? Listen to the answers. Now, hug and kiss the baby and send loving, nurturing, and supportive energy to him/her. Visualise a beautiful pink light surrounding the baby. This is a protective circle of Love. Now allow yourself to merge with this circle of Love making you and the baby one and whole.

## Method 3:

### Write a Letter to Your Inner Child

Take a photo of yourself when you were a child. Look at this photo and write a letter to your inner child. You can write all your wishes, wants and desires. You can write a letter of apology or a letter of forgiveness to your inner child. You can tell your inner child how sorry you are that he/she suffered and were hurt. Tell him or her how wonderful they are, how much you love them and that you are going to protect them now. Tell them it is safe to feel and express your emotions. There is no need to justify or make excuses for the way you feel. Everything is well now and always will be because you are on their side.

## Method 4:

### Visualisation exercises

You can visualise yourself as a child. For example, you relax and imagine the child aspect of yourself. See yourself as a child and ask questions:
- How the child feels
- What the child believes
- What is hurting the child
- What makes him/her happy
- How you can support the child
- How the child wants to be nurtured, treated, and played with?

Listen to the answers ... The answers come from your subconscious mind.

These exercises will help you re-connect with your inner child and heal it. The result will be amazing - it helps you became a good parent by understanding how to love.

## Chakras and Inner Child Healing

The inner child lives in the 1st chakra (the tribal chakra). The 1st chakra is responsible for how safe, secure, supported and protected we feel in the world, in general. Security and dependency are the major issues of the inner child. When we heal our inner child, we restore our safety and security. All chakras are involved and affected by the inner child healing, but the most significant changes occur in the 1st chakra (tribal chakra) and the 2nd chakra (relationships).

Look at the table below and see how each chakra is affected by the inner child healing process.

Inner child healing process.

| Chakra | How it is affected by the Inner Child Healing |
|---|---|
| 1 Chakra - Tribal power | The healing of your inner child makes you feel safe, secure, supported, and protected in every tribe and in every family of your life. |
| 2 Chakra - Relationships | It makes you feel safe and comfortable with your partners – personal and professional. |
| 3 Chakra - Solar Plexus | It helps you love yourself as you are. |
| 4 Chakra - Heart chakra | It helps you experience unconditional love. When you heal your own inner child, you can understand the inner child in other people. |
| 5 Chakra - Throat | It helps you speak your truth without fear of being judged. It allows you to be vulnerable but not feel victimised. |
| 6 Chakra - Third Eye | It helps you see the truth about people and yourself, since you understand the vulnerability of the inner child. |
| 7 Chakra - Divine Connection | It helps you connect with the Divine. The inner child knows that you are always a part of the Divine. |

## Chapter 15:
# INTUITIVE HEALING THROUGH DREAMS, VISIONS AND HYPNAGOGIC STATES

I am a big dreamer and genuinely believe that dreams provide answers about our health, relationships, jobs, and new directions in life. Some dreams are healing. They can bring direct healing when you go to bed sick and wake up feeling much better, or they can provide you with valuable information on how to heal a problem.

During sleep, we are connected to our intuitive mind, which is the biggest part and takes 90-95% of the whole consciousness. The information that is secret to the logic mind is in dreams. The trick is to understand this information and use it.

Look at how much time we spend sleeping:
- at **age 30** we have slept 4339 days (11.9 years)
- at **age 40** we have slept 5556 days (15.2 years)
- at **age 50** we have slept 6773 days (18.6 years)
- at **age 60** we have slept 7990 days (21.9 years)
- at **age 70** we have slept 9207 days (25.2 years)
- at **age 80** we have slept 10424 days (28.6 years)

- at **age 90** we have slept 11641 days (31.9 years)
- at **age 100**, we have slept 12858 days (35.2 years)

We spend 1/3 of our lives sleeping. If you think that sleeping time is just to get unconscious and then wake up – then you may be wasting 1/3 of your life. During sleep we are connected to our intuitive mind and can access what is hidden and secret.

Need an idea? - Just Sleep ...

You do not have to be a psychic reader or a master shaman to access deep intuitive knowledge that can guide you through the most difficult situations.

Look at the most fascinating inventions that are the products of dreams.

1. . Elias Howe's lockstitch sewing machine was a result of his violent murder dream: he was surrounded by cannibals who had spears with holes. This was a symbolic image of his famous invention.
2. James Cameron's, 'Terminator' was a product of his dream.
3. Albert Einstein dreamt about electrocuting cows and then came up with his Theory of Relativity. After contemplating on the problem, he started to put together the idea that events look different depending on where you are standing, because of the time it takes the light to reach your eyes. In other words, the theory of relativity.
4. Paul McCartney wrote, 'Yesterday' in a dream.

5. Mary Shelley's, 'Frankenstein' was inspired by a dream.
6. Dreams lead to Nobel Prize winner - Otto Loewi, a German born physiologist, who won the Nobel Prize for medicine in 1936 for his work on the chemical transmission of nerve impulses.
7. Abraham Lincoln dreamt of his assassination and he described it very precisely before the event happened.
8. Robert Louis Stevenson got his, 'Jekyll and Mr. Hyde' from a dream.
9. Jack Nicklaus found a new golf swing in a dream.
10. Stephen King dreamt his, 'The King of Horror' and some other novels he wrote.

These examples are only a fraction of the great inventions and inspirations that were found in dreams. There are many more, and I cannot put all of them in this book. But you got an idea – if you need new ideas – just dream.

## Healing Dreams

Many dreams are healing. They can bring an instant healing or can give you information about how to heal an illness.

Many neuroscientists believe that the deepest traumas can be healed only in a dream state like lucid dreaming. Lucid dreaming is the awareness of the fact that you are dreaming. When you are aware, you can control the dream, and change the outcome of the events in a dream. I witnessed this kind of healing in Russia, when we had many ex-soldiers arrive back from the Afghanistan war with severe post-traumatic stress disorders which were unresponsive to conventional treatments. The soldiers kept re-experiencing flashbacks and could not adjust to peaceful life. After going through lucid dreaming therapy, many PTSD soldiers got much better. They were put in a sleeping lab, with electrodes on their heads and were taught to identify the time when they experience lucid dreaming. Once they realise this, they had the ability to control their dreams and change the outcome.

Many severe PTSD can be healed using this method. You do not have to be in the lab to use this technique. You can do it at home. You just need to identify the time when you experience lucid dreaming and know what you need to change.

Lucid dreaming technique can help you re-program your negative memories, traumas, habits, addictions, and many other problems.

## How to Experience Lucid Dreaming

1. Keep a dream journal where you record your dreams. Identify common themes in your dreams.
2. Identify the time when you experience lucid dreaming. Lucid dreaming is when you are aware that you are dreaming. When I experience lucid dreaming, I tell myself, "Irina, this is just a dream." It means that I am aware that I am dreaming, and I can control the dream. I usually experience lucid dreaming around 5 a.m.
3. Before going to sleep, identify exactly what you need to heal: a memory, a behaviour, or a trauma.
4. In your dream journal, write down what you need to heal, so you can bring the issue into the dream and change the outcome. You do it just before sleeping.

5. Do not dissipate the energy of your intent. Energy dissipation occurs when you start thinking about something else after making a request. Therefore, after writing down the request, meditate and sense subtle energy in your body. Do not allow any thoughts to enter your mind until you fall asleep. If any thoughts come, say, "Not this thought, not this thought ..." and visualise thoughts flying away from your head as clouds.
6. When you experience lucid dreaming, bring the issue into the dream, and change the outcome to a better one.

**NOTE:** It takes time to work with dreams. First, you need to work with your dream journal and record your dreams, until you become familiar with the themes of your dreams. Then, you can identify the time when you experience lucid dreaming. It is a remarkably interesting exercise and is extremely healing.

## Types of Dreams

I notice that many people complain that their dreams do not make any sense. Some people have nightmares or scary dreams. Often, they become confused about what these dreams mean. They do not have to.

Most of our dreams, about 80% of all dreams are psychological. Psychological dreams **do not predict anything**. They reflect our unexpressed emotions. This is the way our body processes emotions that were suppressed during the day.

Only about 20% of all our dreams can predict something or imply future information.

Here are the types of dreams:
1. Psychological or emotional dreams (about 80% of all dreams we have)
2. Predictive or prophetic dreams (about 10%)
3. Counselling or guiding dreams (about 10%).

## **Psychological or Emotional Dreams**

The major characteristics of psychological dreams are **emotions** during the dream. These dreams make you feel scared, fearful, sad, jealous, exited, happy, powerful etc ... Psychological dreams do not predict anything. They mean that your body is dealing with emotions that you suppressed during the day. These dreams help to process wounds, problems, or any unexpressed feelings - past or present.

Some of the common examples of emotional dreams are:
- Standing naked in front of people – means that you feel vulnerable about certain situations or dealing with other people. Your body is processing this vulnerability.
- Being chased by a monster (or a scary person) – means that you are afraid of certain people or situations and your body is processing this fear.
- Your teeth fall out (cracked or decay) – mean that the source of power has been taken away from you and you cannot bite anymore. Your body is processing the loss of power from relationships, jobs, or other situations.

Most nightmares are psychological dreams. Nightmares do not predict anything; they mean that your body is emotionally overwhelmed. Do not worry when you have nightmares, it is a good thing, your body is dealing with emotions you could not deal with. All you need to do is to calm down, practice energy healing techniques on yourself, and feel grateful that your body is finally processing your trapped feelings.

## Predictive or Prophetic Dreams

Predictive or prophetic dreams are not as common as psychological. In fact, they are rare. The main characteristic of a prophetic dream is neutrality and no emotions in the dream. You experience a witnessing state as if you are watching a movie. The emotional response may come after the dream, but during the dream it feels totally impersonal and detached from you.

Example: some people saw the September 11 attack in their dreams before it happened; but they could not see the details of the event (where and when). This is the characteristic of the prophetic dreams – people see the event but cannot see the details so they cannot warn anybody. They receive general information from the collective consciousness but no specific details of where and when things will happen.

## Counselling or Guiding Dreams

Counselling or guiding dreams are also rare. They provide a concrete advise or counselling about specific situations, problems, or illnesses. Your body feels sensually responsive during these dreams and you feel physical reactions such as goose bumps, the hair on the back of your neck standing on end, choking sensations, or maybe pains or aches anywhere in the body or organs.

Counselling dreams provide you with the inner knowing about how to deal with certain issues. Here you need to remember that genuine intuitive guidance is always compassionate and supportive. Negative or harmful feelings come from fear and they are not genuine guidance.

Fear is not intuitive, it comes from the wound that still needs healing. Be aware of it.

Example of a counselling dream:

> My client told me that once he experienced a 'heart attack' during a dream. He felt a severe pain in his chest and was taken to hospital in a dream. When he woke up, he was physically healthy, but he realised that he must forgive his ex-wife. The wound after divorce was hurting him and interfering with his daily life. Only after experiencing a 'heart attack' in a dream he was able to go through a forgiveness process, and forgave his ex-wife. His dream saved him from having a real heart attack, which he would have got if he did not go through the forgiveness process.

## How to Work with Dreams

I encourage people to work with dreams actively. This means you are not just a passive receiver of what comes in a dream, but an active participant in a dreaming process.

Being a passive receiver means you just see what comes during dreams and then try to make sense of what it means.

You can use dreams in a more effective way.

> You can ask questions and make requests before going to sleep. This is a much better option.

During sleep we are in direct contact with our intuitive mind, which is 90% of our whole mind capacity. Therefore, we can use this time to answer difficult questions, solve problems, heal what is considered 'incurable' etc ...

To do that you need to have a dream journal and every night write down what you want to solve during the night. When you write down a request, you direct your consciousness to the problem and have a good chance of getting the answer.

Another important thing here **is not to dissipate energy** after making a request. This means, you write down a question or make a request, then put your dream journal aside and meditate. Do not allow any thoughts to come in. Thoughts mean energy dissipation. The best practice is to sense subtle energy in your body after making a request. This practice gives you the best chance to receive the answers.

If you did not get any answers, or they were inconclusive, you can ask it again the next night. The guidance will come. Keep asking.

## Hypnagogic State

A hypnagogic state is a transitional state between sleep and wakefulness. Usually we experience this period in the morning. It is a very vulnerable state when we are partially asleep and partially awake. You are still connected to the intuitive mind during the hypnagogic state.

If you know what problems you need to work on, you can bring the issue into the hypnagogic state and explore it. You will be amazed by what kind of information you receive. This information comes from the intuitive mind and it is totally different from the logic mind information.

## How to use Hypnagogic State for Healing and Re-Programming Yourself

1. Identify when you experience the hypnagogic state. For me it is closer to the morning, at about 6 am or just before I wake up.
2. In your dream journal, write down the issue that you need to heal or transform. It should be a specific issue or a question.
3. When you are in hypnagogic state, bring the issue into the state and look at the issue using your intuitive mind.
4. When you wake up - write down the information you received in your dream journal.

## Dreams are the Answers to What you Ask Before you Fall Asleep

I believe that dreams are the most powerful and the most accessible tool to connect to the intuitive mind. In this book I have described three reliable ways to work with dreams:
1. Ask questions or make requests before you go to sleep and record the answer in morning.
2. Work with lucid dreaming.
3. Work with hypnagogic states.

All these techniques are enormously powerful tools. Try them and master at least one of them. You will not be disappointed. It will become the most reliable tool you can use to get genuine intuitive guidance for any life situation. It always tells the truth.

## Chapter 16:
# INTUITIVE EATING - HEALING WITH FOOD

When I was a young woman, I suffered from a severe eating disorder. I fluctuated from bulimia to anorexia, back and forth, for nearly two decades. None of the conventional approaches or diets helped me to improve my health until I discovered Intuitive eating. Intuitive eating is understanding that you are the expert of your own body and its hunger signals. If you listen to your intuition, it tells you what to eat, when to eat, how much to eat.

Eating is an instinct that is a part of our intuitive voice. When we follow diets, we disregard our intuitive voice and follow someone's else suggestions instead.

The trick here is to differentiate genuine eating instincts from the voices of addictions, compulsions, and cravings. My eating disorder significantly improved when I managed to separate the voice of addiction, (that told me to binge-purge or starve myself) from my genuine inner voice. You can read how to differentiate the voices of intuition from the voices of fear and brain chatter in the chapter, 'How to Differentiate Intuition from Fear, Brain Chatter and other False Perceptions.'

## Food Intuitions

Genuine intuitions about food come from the solar plexus (gut instincts). To feel intuitions about food, first of all you should learn to feel calmness inside. The calmness inside is achieved with meditation: Body scan meditation, or chakras scan meditation. The calmer you become – the more you can feel your genuine eating instincts.

I have also noticed that a short mediation before eating helps to hear eating instincts while eating. It prevents you from overeating and binging food. I recommend a two-minute meditation just before you begin to eat.

## Two-Minute Meditation Before Eating a Meal

1. Sit straight and take a deep breath in and out.
2. Stop all the thoughts. If any thoughts come, say: "Not this thought. Not this thought." And visualise thoughts flow away from your head as clouds.

> 3. Focus on the middle part of your body while breathing.
> 4. Feel the air flow down to the base of your spine and then, up to your head.
> 5. Do this breathing for two-minutes, then you can start eating.

This two-minute meditation helps to align your chakras just before eating. Chakras are in the middle of the body. By breathing through the middle, you align your chakras. It helps to feel calmness inside and sense the eating instincts more.

Another way to feel calmness inside is to do energetic cleansing of your solar plexus before eating. Do it for two-minutes before you begin to eat.

## Two-minute Solar Plexus Cleansing before you Begin to Eat

> 1. Sit straight and take a deep breath.
> 2. Rub your hands together for a few seconds until they become warm.
> 3. Spread your hands apart and feel as if you are holding an 'energy ball.'
> 4. Focus on your hands and feel 'tingling and crawling' sensations inside your hands. This means your hands are ready to sense energy.
> 5. Bring your right hand, if you are right-handed, 20 cm from your solar plexus. Find the edge of the solar plexus aura.

6. Start anticlockwise movements with your right hand as if you are scooping ice-cream from a tub.
7. Scoop the energy from your solar plexus and throw it into a fire, (a candle). If you do not have a candle, visualise a flame in front of you. Always burn the removed energy.
8. Do this for two-minutes, then start eating the meal.

## How to Clean and Energise your Food

To maintain energetic purity inside and around you, it is a good idea to clean your food and energise it before eating. All food has energy. Food contains the energy of the ingredients and the energy of the people who cooked, packed, and prepared the food. You can clean it. Here are the steps.

### How to Clean your Food before Eating

1. Rub your hands together for thirty seconds until they are warm.
2. Spread your hands about 20 cm (7 inches) apart and feel the energy ball.
3. You should feel 'tingling and crawling' sensations in your hands. This means that your hands are ready to sense energy.
4. Bring your hands about 20 cm (7 inches) above your food.

> 5. Find the edge of the aura that comes from the food. It feels like an energy current above the food. It is very subtle.
> 6. Start **anticlockwise movements** with your hands. Check the direction with a watch: Apply a watch face up above the food.
> 7. Do anticlockwise movements for one-minute or until you feel pure vibrations.
> 8. Say a mantra: "Clean, clean, clean …"

After cleansing the food, you can energise it with positive energy.

## How to Energise your Food

Energising food means putting positive energy into the food before eating it.

> 1. Rub your hands together for a few seconds until they are warm.
> 2. Spread them 20 cm (7 inches) apart and feel the energy ball.
> 3. Visualise a brilliant light enters the space between your hands.
> 4. Now you are holding a brilliant energy ball.
> 5. Bring this energy ball to your food – 20 cm (7 inches) above it.
> 6. Start **clockwise movements** with your hands.
> 7. Visualise the brilliant energy going inside the food.

> 8. Do clockwise movements with your hands for one minute.
> 9. Say the mantra: "Energise, energise, energise …"
> 10. Eat the cleaned and energised food.

Cleansing and energising food promotes health and wellbeing as it makes you aware of the energy inside you and the energy you are going to take in with the food. The rule to remember is that first you need to do cleansing, (energy out), then energising (energy in).

## Energetic Meaning of Food

My eating disorder has taught me, that food has a special spiritual role. Food changes our energy. Therefore, we must listen to the still, subtle voice within us that knows exactly what we need to eat, when we need to eat and how much we need to eat. It is the voice of our intuition - our deepest truth that always knows what we need in our body, mind, and soul.

When I was working on healing my eating disorder, I recorded how different foods made me feel and how my emotions influenced my food choices. Here is the list of connections between food, emotions, and beliefs which I created because of my challenge. These food-emotion connections are perfectly accurate because I tested them on hundreds of my patients and clients.

So, what it means to have cravings for:

**Dairy (milk, ice cream, cheese):** Craving for Unconditional Love. Our first food was milk—mother's milk. We remember it for life. When we feel we are not receiving these desirable feelings of Love - we crave dairy products and milk.

**What should you do?** – Learn to love life and life experiences unconditionally. It is not about having a romantic partner but about loving life as a process of life. Follow the spiritual truth, 'Love is Divine Power' – 4$^{th}$ chakra.

Say to yourself: "I love and approve of myself. I love my Life."

**Chocolate:** This is a substitute for romantic love and physical pleasure. We are all sensual, sexual beings. Eating chocolate produces the same feelings in the body as having a romance. It is also a substitute for sex and physical contacts such as kissing and hugging.

**What should you do?** – Acknowledge your emotional needs and try to get joy by actively participating in life experiences. You can experience physical pleasure from exercising, meditating, expressing your creativity such as dressing up, decorating, writing, singing, dancing etc … Say to yourself: " I love my life, I love my body. I am a good partner to myself."

**Alcohol:** Problems with acceptance. Thinking: "I will not be accepted for who I am." Alcohol can provide the illusion of self-acceptance. It can also protect you from the perceived dangers of intimacy. Bubbly drinks, such as champagne, can be used as a substitute for excitement.

**What should you do?** - Acknowledge the real reasons why you drink and try to heal it using energy healing techniques. Most alcoholics respond well when they follow the spiritual truth, 'Surrender your personal will to Divine will' – the 5$^{th}$ chakra. It means they separate the voices of their addiction (personal will) from the voices of the Divine and follow the Divine will.

Use this affirmation: "I love each moment of my life. I love the NOW. I love myself."

**Salty foods**: Suppressing fear of change and individuation. Afraid to take risk or fear rejection. Afraid to be different in a group.

**What should you do?** – Acknowledge your hidden fears and release them from your body using energy healing techniques.

Use this affirmation: "I am safe, secure, supported and protected. I am safe to be me."

**Sugar:** Craving for excitement and sweetness. We are supposed to get 'sweetness' from our life experiences and other people. When we feel that we are not getting 'sweetness' from our relationships – we use sugar instead. Sugar becomes a substitute for a playmate.

**What should you do?** – Acknowledge your emotional needs and try to get joy by actively participating in life experiences. Become your own best friend by understanding different parts of yourself.

Use this affirmation: "My life is sweet. I love my life. I love myself."

**Crunchy foods:** Trying to supress anger, avoiding anger, acting out of anger in a safe way. Dealing with people or circumstances causing us to be angry, but in a subtle way.

**What should you do?** – Understand who and what makes you angry and release anger using energy healing techniques. Follow the spiritual truth, 'Honour One Another' – the 2$^{nd}$ chakra, which means we should not go into a relationship if we do not honour the other person or the other person does not honour us.

Use this affirmation: "I trust the process of life. Life supports and loves me."

**High-gluten or wheat products:** Craving for comfort and safety. What is more comforting than a warm cinnamon roll, mashed potatoes, or a bowl of pasta? Gluten products give us the comfort and safety we need in a non-threatening way. Has a cinnamon roll ever rejected you?

*What should you do?* – Acknowledge your needs for inner comfort and try to feel comfortable with who you are and where you are. Follow the spiritual truths, "All is One" and "Honour Yourself."

Use this affirmation: "I am safe, secure, supported and protected. I love my life."

**Fatty foods:** Dealing with shame and protection. Fatty foods provide a protection from shame and guilt. Fat is a buffer to protect us from the energy of other people.

*What should you do?* – Acknowledge your needs for protection and release the feelings of shame from your body using energy healing techniques. Follow the spiritual truths, "All is One" and "Honour One Another."

Use this affirmation: "I am safe, secure, supported and protected. I trust the process of life."

**Corn:** Craving for success in personal and professional life. Feeling that I am not successful the way I am. Eating corn can bring instant feelings of success.

*What should you do?* – Acknowledge that true success comes from being yourself! Say to yourself: "I love and approve of myself. My life is a successful journey and I love it."

## How Food Influences Chakras

Food influences our consciousness and our chakras (energy centres). All foods vibrate and these vibrations change our energy.

Different foods can increase or decrease chakra vibrations. Over the years I have collected lists of foods that increase or decrease the energy of chakras. Here are the lists for each chakra.

## *Chakra One (The Tribal)*

### To Increase the Vibrations of the 1st Chakra:
- red meat
- animal fats
- coffees and colas
- spinach, beets, grapes, strawberries, and cherries

Emotional Message of these foods: I deserve to be alive, safe, strong, and passionate.

### To Decrease the Vibrations of the 1st Chakra:
(if it is overstimulated)
- Avoid the foods above and eat more light colour foods such as green pears, green apples, cauliflower, white nectarines, and white peaches.

## *Chakra Two (The Sacral)*

### To Increase the Vibrations of the 2nd Chakra:
- Chocolate
- Salmon
- Fruits such as orange and papaya
- Vegetables such as sweet potatoes, pumpkins
- Honey
- Pastas and other wheat foods

- Ice cream
- Milk and dairy products
- Bread and butter

Emotional Message of these foods: I am feeling attractive, desired, and desirable.

**To Decrease the Vibrations of the 2nd Chakra:**
(if it is overstimulated)

- Avoid the foods above and eat more cold colour foods such as cucumbers, turnips, cauliflower, squash, white radish etc ...

## *Chakra Three (The Solar Plexus)*

**To Increase the Vibrations of the 3rd Chakra:**
- Corn
- Fish and chicken
- Apricots, carrots, sweet potatoes
- Grapefruit and squashes.

Emotional Message of these foods: I deserve success because I am intelligent, capable, and strong.

**To Decrease the Vibrations of the 3rd Chakra:**
(if it is overstimulated)
- Avoid the foods above and eat more cold colour foods – the same as per chakra two.

## Chakra Four (The Heart)

### To Increase the Vibrations of the 4th Chakra:
- Green foods, such as vegetables and sauces
- Plums and cherries
- Miso, soy, and bean proteins
- Grains and nuts.

Spiritual Message of these foods: "I am loved and loveable. I love my life."

### To Decrease the Vibrations of the 4th Chakra:
(if it is overstimulated)
- Avoid the foods above. Drink more fresh juices, mineral water, and herbal teas.

## Chakra Five (The Throat)

### To Increase the Vibrations of the 5th Chakra:
- Blue foods, such as berries.
- All spices, which stimulate the mouth.
- Ginseng
- Reishi mushrooms
- Barley and wheat grass
- Echinacea
- Kelp.

Emotional Message of these foods: "I am honest and true to myself. I can manifest my needs. It is safe to communicate."

**To Decrease the Vibrations of the 5th Chakra:**
(if it is overstimulated)
- Avoid the foods above. Drink more water and herbal teas.

## *Chakra Six (The Third Eye)*

**To Increase the Vibrations of the 6th Chakra:**
- Purple foods, such as grapes and eggplants
- Lecithin
- Wheat germ
- Chamomile
- Alfalfa.

Emotional Message of these foods: "I am acceptable as I am. I see the truth and make healthy choices."

**To Decrease the Vibrations of the 6th Chakra:**
(if it is overstimulated)
- Avoid the foods above. Drink more water and detox yourself.

## *Chakra Seven (The Crown)*

**To Increase the Vibrations of the 7th Chakra:**
- Water
- Sacred herbs, including sage and lemongrass.

Emotional Message of these foods: "I have a unique destiny. I know and follow my purpose. I am connected to the Divine."

## Chapter 17:
# HOW TO FORGIVE

I love the topic of forgiveness and always include it in my books, talks, and workshops. I believe that forgiveness is not just important for our health; it is absolutely necessary for it. In fact, without forgiveness we cannot heal ...

Over the years, I have met many people who asked me similar questions such as, "Irina, I have studied spirituality for many years. Why I am not healing?"

A common reason for not being able to heal properly is the inability to forgive and let go.

So, how can we truly forgive?

Forgiveness cannot be achieved with elevated thoughts or strong intentions alone. It comes about by engaging certain practical tools that release your body, mind, and soul, from the trapped wounded energy that has caused you to feel so much pain and then be able to replace it with new healing energy instead.

When we forgive, we release our hurts, grow from it, and become better people. Every experience in life teaches us a lesson and only forgiveness can make us learn the lesson properly. Only true forgiveness will make us heal. In fact, healing is a journey of forgiveness. When I talked about the Heart chakra,

I explained the differences between true forgiveness and fake forgiveness.

The essential things that forgiveness brings are self-love and self-acceptance.

This means that you can accept yourself and your life fully, with all your experiences, situations, and circumstances.

Forgiveness means that you can look back at your life and say: **"Everything is as it should be. Nothing could have been or should have been any different."**

You feel grateful for all the challenges, because through these challenges you became the person you are right now ... This is true forgiveness ... Only at this level will we begin to heal and love life again.

## The Steps to Forgiveness

Here are the steps to forgiveness. For a better result you should forgive one person at a time.

Follow these steps:

1. Call for Divine help, say: "Intuitive Healing Power, I call on you to come to me and help me forgive. I call on my Soul and my Higher self. I call on my guides, teachers and angels who love me unconditionally. Thank you for your unconditional love, support, and protection.

   Thank you, Thank you, Thank you ..."

2. Connect yourself to the Divine pillar of light: This starts from the Divine (cosmos, universe) and enters your body through the top of your head. Feel the energy of this Divine pillar of light entering your body through the top of your head. Meditate on this connection for two to three minutes.

3. Think about the person you need to forgive: Visualise him/her.
4. Say, "I call on the spirit of ... (name of the person)." Call three times.
5. Say, "Thank you for being here and clearing our energy today."
6. Say, "(Name), I now forgive you for everything that you have ever done to me that has hurt me in this or any other lifetime. I forgive you; I forgive you; I forgive you ..." Breathe in and release.

Repeat this step three times.

7. Now attend to the other side of situation: What you may have done to them. Say: "(Their name), I now ask that you forgive me for everything that I have ever done that has hurt you consciously or unconsciously in this or any other lifetime. Please forgive me, please forgive me and please forgive me." Breathe in and release.

Repeat this step three times.

8. Imagine lines of energy joining you to the other person. Raise your hand and bring it down like cutting the ties and say, "I set myself free and reclaim my spirit now. I proclaim that all karma between us ended by my sincere act of forgiveness. May you be free and may all good things happen to you. Thank you, thank you, thank you ..." Breathe in and release.

Repeat this step three times.

**9.** Give thanks to Divine: Say, "Intuitive Healing Power thank you, thank you, thank you ..." Breathe in and release.

Repeat this step three times.

Forgiveness will empower you and heal you. Forgiveness is unconditional love that will make you strong, powerful, and enlightened.

**Note:** Often, the person you need to forgive the most is you. Forgiving yourself is no different to forgiving another person. You need to go through the same process and follow the same steps. Visualise yourself as you would visualise any other person. When you need to cut the energy line, cut the energy line between the version of you who caused the problems and the new version of you who is asking for forgiveness.

## How Does Forgiveness Affect Chakras?

All chakras are affected by the Forgiveness process, but the most significant changes occur in the 4$^{th}$ chakra (heart chakra). The Forgiveness process will rise you from the area below the belt, (lower- self chakras, conditional love chakras) to the area above the belt, (higher-self chakras, unconditional love chakras).

Look at the table below and see how each chakra is affected by the Forgiveness process.

| Chakra | How it is Affected by Forgiveness |
|---|---|
| 1 Chakra - Tribal power | Forgiveness makes you understand the spiritual truth of the 1st chakra, "All is One," or, "All for One and One for All." |
| 2 Chakra - Relationships | Forgiveness makes you understand the spiritual truth of the 2nd chakra, "Honour One Another." |
| 3 Chakra - Solar Plexus | Forgiveness makes you understand the spiritual truth of the 3rd chakra, "Honour Yourself." |
| 4 Chakra - Heart chakra | Forgiveness makes you understand the spiritual truth of the 4th chakra, "Love is Divine Power," which is about Unconditional Love. |
| 5 Chakra - Throat | Forgiveness makes you understand the spiritual truth of the 5th chakra, "Surrender Your Personal Will to Divine Will." |
| 6 Chakra - Third Eye | Forgiveness makes you understand the spiritual truth of the 6th chakra, "Seek only the Truth." You can only see the truth when you release your emotions about the situation – when you truly Forgive. |
| 7 Chakra - Divine Connection | Forgiveness makes you understand the spiritual truth of the 7th chakra, "Stay in the Present Moment." We are the most powerful when we release the past burdens, do not worry about the future, and truly embrace the present moment. |

## Chapter 18:
# CHARTING YOUR PROGRESS

This book is not just a book but a healing guide. It takes you through the process of self-discovery and understanding your own health. Now reflect on your experiences by answering these questions. Chart your own progress ...

1. How many days this week did you scan your own chakras by doing the Chakra Scan Meditation? (I hope by now you realised the value of the scan) .......................................................

2. Have you answered the chakras questions in the chapter 5? ........................................................................................

3. Which chakras do you have problems with according to the test?........................................................................................

4. Have you cleaned your own chakras? What did you feel when doing the cleansing process? .......................................

5. Have you cleaned your own aura? What did you feel when doing aura cleansing on yourself? ......................................

6. Have you re-created your own aura following the aura re-creation technique? What did you feel during the process? ..................................................................................

7. Which chakra in your body is the easiest to connect to? (this would be your strongest chakra) ........................................

8. Which chakra feels like your favourite and why? (this would be the chakra that you keep developing) ........................

9. Which organs in your body are the easiest to connect to? ..................................................................................

10. What organs in your body do you feel as your strongest? ..................................................................................

11. What organs in your body do you feel as your weakest? What did you do to strengthen them energetically? ..................................................................................

12. Have you tried to remove the energy of illness from your organs using the intuitive healing techniques? What organs did you work with? What did you feel during and after the process? ........................................................................

13. Have you identified the emotional/energetic meaning of your health problems? ........................................................

14. Have you started to record your dreams in a dream journal? ..................................................................................

15. Have you asked questions and made requests in your dream journal before going to sleep? ....................................

16. Have you received the answers you were looking for? ..................................................................................

17. Have you tried to identify the time when you experience lucid dreaming? ................................................................

18. Have you experienced psychological dreams? How often do you have them? What hidden feelings and emotions do they reflect? ................................................................

19. Have you experienced counselling dreams? What did they guide you to do? ................................................................

20. Have you experienced predictive dreams? What did they predict? ................................................................

21. Have you tried to identify the time when you experienced a hypnagogic state? ................................................................

22. Have you tried to use lucid dreaming and hypnagogic states to heal your problems using the techniques you have learned here? ................................................................

23. Have you tried intuitive eating – listening to your intuition about what and when you should eat instead of following diets? ................................................................

24. How easy is it for you to differentiate intuition from the voices of fear and brain chatter? ................................................................

25. Have you tried to experience the Internal Smile technique? What did you feel during the process? ................................................................

26. Have you tried the intuitive healing techniques on your partner? What was the result? ................................................................

27. Have you dealt with your Inner Child? Have you tried to connect to your Inner Child using the intuitive healing techniques? ................................................................

28. Have you done the forgiveness process? Who did you forgive? Do you need to do it again? ...................................................

29. Have you forgiven yourself? ...........................................................

# INTUITIVE HEALING TABLES

## Table 1:
### Organ Meanings

This table provides only short descriptions of the emotional meaning of organs. If you are interested in learning more about it, please read my book, "The Secret Energy of Your Body: An Intuitive Guide to Healing, Health and Wellness."

The emotional meaning of organs is linked to the chakra – organ connection. Each organ connects to a chakra (s) and the emotional issues within the chakras.

I started collecting the connections of organs – emotions in Russia when I was doing my specialisation in Immunology – Allergy and became interested in Psychoneuroimmunology. It was around 1995 when I started. Since then, I read many neuroscientific researches completed by many universities all over the world that proved the intuitive connections between organs-symptoms and emotions.

| Organ | Emotional Meaning of the Problems | Affirmation to Heal |
|---|---|---|
| Abdomen | How you digest life and life experiences. | I digest life with ease and grace. I trust life. |

# HOW TO HEAL USING INTUITIVE HEALING

| Organ | Emotional Meaning of the Problems | Affirmation to Heal |
|---|---|---|
| Adrenal glands | How much you love and care for yourself. | I am worthy of good things and good life. |
| Ankles | Directions, flexibility, and pleasure in life. | I lovingly participate in life experiences. |
| Anus | Releasing what is no longer needed. | I release the old and let go with ease. |
| Arms | How you embrace life. Giving and receiving. | I give and receive Love equally. |
| Arteries | How much joy and love do you feel in your life. | I love my life. Joy flows through me. |
| Back | How supported and protected you feel in general. | I am safe, secure, supported and protected. |
| Bladder | Letting go and forgiving your partners and yourself. | I forgive myself and others. I let go with ease. |
| Bones | How safe you feel. | I am safe. I care for myself as much as I care for others. |
| Bowels | Your ability to release the old and let go in life. | I am reborn every moment. I am a new baby again. |
| Brain | How you interpret the information you receive. Self-talk. | I think and feel with Love. |
| Breasts | Nurturing yourself and others. | I nurture myself as much as I nurture others. |

| Organ | Emotional Meaning of the Problems | Affirmation to Heal |
|---|---|---|
| Buttocks | Your own power in face-to-face, one to one relationship. | I am powerful, courageous, and strong. I am safe and protected. |
| Cervix | How comfortable you feel as a woman. | I love being a woman. My power is always with me. |
| Chest | How you balance your emotions with the emotions of other people. | I balance my emotions with ease and grace. |
| Coccyx (tailbone) | Self-sabotage. Feeling unsafe about relationships or money. | I trust the flow of life. I am safe. |
| Ears (problems) | Not trusting what you hear. | I balance what I hear with Love. |
| Elbows | How you look after yourself. | I take care of myself with ease and grace. |
| Eyes | How you balance what you see and what you feel about it. | I balance what I see with Love. |
| Face | How you feel about yourself. What you show to the world. | I am beautiful, loving, and graceful. |
| Fallopian Tubes | Inner child problems. | I love my Inner Child. |
| Feet | Directions in life. Belonging. | I trust my journey. I am safe. I am loved. |
| Fingers | Small details of life. | I balance the details of my life with ease and grace. |

| Organ | Emotional Meaning of the Problems | Affirmation to Heal |
|---|---|---|
| Gall bladder | Supressed anger. | I release the past and express myself with Love. |
| Gums | Making decisions. | I am a decisive person. |
| Hair | Connections, freedom, and personal strength. Tension. | I am strong and free. |
| Hands | How you handle things. | I handle things with love and joy. |
| Head | Balancing spiritual and physical aspects of life. | I easily balance physical and emotional. I am not attached to anything. |
| Heart | How you balance love and security. | I am safe and secure with Love. I am free. |
| Heels (problems) | Tiptoe around others. | I walk with confidence and joy. |
| Hips | How you feel about moving forward in life. | I move forward easily. I know my place in life. |
| Immune system (problems) | Inner conflict. The conflict between inner needs and external pressure. | I am in perfect balance. My needs are met. |
| Jaw (problems) | Cannot bite anymore. Power losses due to relationships. | I release the old and forgive. I regain my power through peace and love. |
| Joints (problems) | Caring for others more than caring for yourself. | I care for myself as much as I care for others. |

| Organ | Emotional Meaning of the Problems | Affirmation to Heal |
|---|---|---|
| Kidneys (problems) | Ancient sadness and grief, (come from the tribe and ancestors) | I release the past and forgive. I live in the present moment. |
| Knees (problems) | Personal pride. Feeling stuck in a pattern that should be released. | I allow my life to flow. I forgive and move on easily. |
| Large intestines | Digesting life and life experiences. Fear. | I am fearless, courageous, and strong. I love myself. |
| Legs | Moving forward. Confidence. | I am moving forward with ease. I love my journey. |
| Liver (problems) | Suppressed anger. | I am at peace with myself and others. I balance life easily. |
| Lungs (problems) | Balancing your own emotions with the emotions of other people. | I balance my emotions easily. I am in a total balance. |
| Mouth (problems) | Expressing disappointments in personal relationships. | I speak my truth easily and effortlessly. I know what I need. |
| Muscles | Your ability to act and follow your higher self. | I am strong, courageous, and powerful. |
| Nails | Your sensitivity and vulnerability. | I am comfortable, secure, and safe. |
| Neck | Congruency and flexibility. Connection between the heart and the mind. | What I feel, what I think and what I speak are the same. I am a congruent person. |

| Organ | Emotional Meaning of the Problems | Affirmation to Heal |
|---|---|---|
| Nervous system | How you receive and process information from the external world. | I am in peace and harmony with the whole of life. |
| Nose | Self-recognition. Self-worth. | I recognise my own self-worth. I am worthy. |
| Oesophagus (problems) | Cannot swallow the problems anymore. | I love and approve of myself. I am at peace and total harmony with the world. |
| Ovaries | How you feel as a woman. Your capacity to create. | I create with Love. I am proud to be a woman. |
| Pancreas (problems) | Issues of responsibility and self-worth. | I am worthy of good things. I love and approve of myself. |
| Penis | Self-worth as a man. | I love myself as I am. I love my life. Life loves me back. |
| Pineal glands (problems) | Do not follow your intuition. Disconnected from the higher self. | I am on the right path. I listen to my intuition and follow it. |
| Pituitary glands (problems) | You are deviated from your spiritual path. Confused about life. | I balance my thoughts and feelings with ease. I follow my intuition. |
| Prostate gland | Masculine strength. Sex and money issues. | I love myself at any age. I am safe to be me. |
| Rib cage (problems) | Self-sabotage. | I listen to my heart and trust it. |
| Shins (problems) | Feeling betrayed and not safe. | I am safe, secure, supported and protected. |

| Organ | Emotional Meaning of the Problems | Affirmation to Heal |
|---|---|---|
| Shoulders | Burdens in life. Taking too much responsibility for others. | I am moving with ease and grace. I am free. |
| Sinuses (problems) | Feeling irritated by other people. | I am in total harmony with everybody and myself. |
| Skeleton | Structure and balance in life. | I have a strong foundation. I am safe. |
| Skin | Safety and protection in life. | I am safe, secure, and supported. I love my life. |
| Small intestine | Fears about life experiences. Not able to take responsibility. | I am strong and courageous. I implement my decisions easily. |
| Spine | How you feel about general sense of support in life. | I am safe and supported. Life supports me. |
| Spleen | Issues of responsibility, obsessions, and addictions. | I trust my life. I love my life. I am worthy. |
| Stomach | Digesting life and life experiences. Fear. | I flow easily with life and life experiences. Life loves me. |
| Teeth | Ability to bite. Making decisions. | I am a decisive person. I follow through my decisions. |
| Testicles | Masculine power. | I love myself as I am. I am safe. |
| Thalamus | Feeling disconnected from 'mother nature.' | I am connected to the natural rhythms of life. |

# HOW TO HEAL USING INTUITIVE HEALING

| Organ | Emotional Meaning of the Problems | Affirmation to Heal |
|---|---|---|
| Thighs | Relationship. Control. Ability to stand your ground or walk away. | I am in my own power. I am safe and secure to be me. |
| Throat | Speaking your truth. | I speak my truth with ease. |
| Thymus gland | Self-sabotage. | I follow my intuition. I love myself. |
| Thyroid glands | Feeling intuitions but not able to express them because of the fear to disturb other people. | I am true to myself and my own nature. I communicate truthfully. I express myself with Love. |
| Toes | Directions in life. | I follow the right directions. Life agrees with me. |
| Tongue | Ability to experience pleasure and sweetness from life experiences. | My life is sweet and pleasurable. I create pleasures for myself. |
| Tonsils | Blocking your creativity. Supressed emotions. | I am a creative person. I express myself with ease and joy. |
| Uterus | Creativity. Fertility. Relationships and money. | I create with Love. My life is beautiful and abundant. |
| Vagina | Vulnerability in relationships. Worthiness of love. | I am worthy of Love. I love myself. I am a strong person. |
| Veins | Experiencing love and joy in life. | I flow with love and joy in my life. |
| Wrist | Handling things. | I handle things with love. |

# Table 2:

## Symptoms and Illnesses Meanings

This table provides only short descriptions of the meanings of symptoms and illnesses. If you are interested in learning more about it, please read my book, "The Secret Energy of Your Body: An Intuitive Guide to Healing, Health and Wellness."

The emotional meaning of symptoms (illnesses) is linked to the chakra – organs connection. Each organ connects to a chakra (s) and the emotional issues within the chakras.

The connections between symptoms and emotions are proven by Psychoneuroimmunology which I have been interested in since 1995 and collected the data that I put in this table.

| Symptom | Emotional Meaning | Affirmations to Heal |
|---|---|---|
| Abdominal cramps. | Feeling stuck in a situation you don't like. | I trust the process of life. I am calm and peaceful with what is. |
| Abscess | Bottling up anger and feeling hurt. | I surrender the outcome to the Divine. Everything will be fine. |
| Accidents | Feeling overwhelmed by negative brain chatter or stress. | I trust life. I am calm, peaceful, and centred. |
| Acid reflux | Not liking your situation and wanting to find the way out. | My life is beautiful. I flow with life nicely. |
| Acne | Feeling uncomfortable in your own skin, unloved, rejected, and unworthy. | I love myself. I love my life. I love all things and people around me. |

| Symptom | Emotional Meaning | Affirmations to Heal |
|---|---|---|
| Acrophobia | Fear of falling down. | I am strong and courageous. I feel calm at the top. |
| Addiction | Trying to numb pain, stress, and anxiety. | I am a beautiful and wonderful person. I enjoy being me. |
| Addison's disease | Too much stress, worries and anxiety. Always busy and having no time for rest. | I love myself. I love my body. I think of myself nicely. |
| Adenoids | Difficulty expressing your own needs due to family friction and arguments. | I speak my truth. I am free to be me. |
| Aging (fear of) | Holding on to the old way of thinking and wrong social beliefs about aging. | I don't think about physical age. I am always young in my spirit. |
| Agoraphobia | Fear of losing control, not trusting others. | I am free and powerful. The energy of others does not affect me. |
| AIDS | Feeling guilty, hopeless, helpless, defenceless, and dirty. | I love my life. I am powerful. I am free. |
| Alcoholism | Self-rejection. | I love and approve of myself. My life has meaning. I know that I belong here. |
| Allergies | Irritated and annoyed with your tribe. | I am safe and free. The energy of others doesn't affect me. |

| Symptom | Emotional Meaning | Affirmations to Heal |
|---|---|---|
| Alzheimer's disease. | Wanting to forget the past. | I forgive myself and others. Every day is a new beginning. |
| Amenorrhea | Uncomfortable with your femininity. | I love being a woman. I am beautiful, feminine, and wonderful all the time. |
| Amnesia | Wanting to forget the past. | I am safe, secure, supported and protected. |
| Anaemia | Forgot how to enjoy life. | I enjoy every day of my life. I love my life. |
| Anal abscess | Having too many repressed fears. | I release the past and move on easily. I forgive myself and others. |
| Anal bleeding | Forcing things to happen rather than letting them happen. | I flow nicely with life. Life continues effortlessly for me. |
| Aneurism | Resisting change. | I surrender the outcome to the Divine. Everything goes as it should. |
| Angina | Lack of intimacy in relationships. | I love my life. I love myself. I treat myself nicely. |
| Anorexia | Extreme denial of self-love and self-nourishment, self-nurturing. | I accept myself and others. I am happy to be me. |
| Anxiety | Living in the past or in the future. | I trust my life. Everything happens as it should. I live in the now. |

## HOW TO HEAL USING INTUITIVE HEALING

| Symptom | Emotional Meaning | Affirmations to Heal |
|---|---|---|
| Appendicitis | Fear of losing power. | I am safe, secure, and supported. I flow nicely with life. |
| Arteriosclerosis | Resisting life and experiencing too much tension and thinking. | I let joy run through my system. I trust love and joy in my life. |
| Arthritis | Too much criticising and judging. | I am free to be me. I am safe. |
| Asperger's syndrome | Cannot fit in. | I am free to be me. Life loves me. |
| Asthma | Feeling smothered, vulnerable, stifled, and suffocated. | I am free and safe. Peace and harmony are within me and around me. |
| Astigmatism | Disliking what you see. | I see with Love. |
| Athlete's foot | Irritated, annoyed, and angry with others. | I am in total balance with myself and others. |
| Attention deficit disorder | Feeling trapped in your own environment. | I am a part of the Divine. Life loves me. |
| Autism | Feeling isolated, imprisoned, frustrated and helpless. | I am loved the way I am. Life loves me. |
| Bacterial infection | Hiding emotions inside rather than expressing them. | I am letting go the past. Only Love flows through me. |
| Bad breath | Feeling frustrated, rejected, irritated and uncomfortable with yourself. | I love and respect myself. I am worthy. |

| Symptom | Emotional Meaning | Affirmations to Heal |
|---|---|---|
| Baldness | Holding on to fear and tension. | I am calm, relaxed, and peaceful. I flow nicely in life. |
| Bed wetting | Feeling scared of some family members or authorities. | I am safe, secure, supported and protected. I am loved. |
| Bell's palsy | Experiencing too much strain, resisting, and pushing rather than going with the flow. | I love the process of life. I go with the flow. |
| Bi-polar disorder (Manic Depression) | Repressed childhood issues. | My health is independent of my family history. I create my own life. |
| Birth defects | Karmic choice to teach parents lessons of love, humility, and compassion. | This child is pure Love. Everything is a blessing in its own way. |
| Blackheads (Pimples) | Angry with yourself and others. Uncomfortable being yourself. | I love and approve of myself. I am safe to be me. |
| Bladder cancer | Experiencing internal conflict: Who you are and what you should be doing in life. | I am at peace with myself. I release the old and welcome a new life. |
| Bleeding | Letting your joy run away from you. | I flow in life with joy. |
| Bleeding gums | Inability to express your needs and feelings. | I know what I want. I have the power to communicate freely. |

# HOW TO HEAL USING INTUITIVE HEALING

| Symptom | Emotional Meaning | Affirmations to Heal |
| --- | --- | --- |
| Blindness | Not wanting to see the world around you. | I see with Love. |
| Blisters | Pushing over your limit and not listening to your body. | I am gentle with myself. I listen to my body. |
| Bloating | Holding on to anger, self-doubting, blame, self-sabotage. | I let go easily. I choose to love myself. |
| Blood clotting | Resisting the flow of life. | Every day is a new day. I flow with the new experiences effortlessly. |
| Body odour | Dislike of the self. | I love myself. I love my body. |
| Boils | Internal resentment and unexpressed anger. | I am at peace with my life. Only love flows through me. |
| Bone cancer | Holding on to pain, resentment, and childhood problems. | I am my own authority. I feel and think independently from everybody else. |
| Bone deformity | Going against your beliefs and following wrong directions. | I trust the flow of life. Everything has a Divine reason. |
| Bone morrow problems | Loss of faith and directions in life. | I am Divinely supported. Life loves me. |
| Bone break | Reaching breaking point in your life. | I can heal my life. Every end is a new beginning. |
| Bone weakness | Feeling unsupported, weak, unsure, limited. | I am safe, secure, supported and protected. |

| Symptom | Emotional Meaning | Affirmations to Heal |
|---|---|---|
| Brain tumour | Experiencing internal conflict and stuck in negative thinking. | I am thinking with Love. Only Love flows through my mind. |
| Breast cancer | Lack of self-love, self-nurturing and self-appreciation. | I care for myself as much as I care for others. I am important and deserve my own Love. |
| Breast cysts/lumps | Lack of self-nurturing. | I nurture myself with Love. |
| Breastfeeding (inability) | Feeling inadequate in a current situation. | I am a good mother. I enjoy the experience. |
| Bronchitis | Carrying family conflicts inside your chest. | I am in compete harmony with myself and others. I am at peace. |
| Bruises | Believing in pain and punishment | I am loving and gentle with myself. I nurture myself with Love. |
| Bulimia | Self-denial, self-punishment, and self-sabotage. | Life loves and co-operates with me. I trust the process of life. |
| Bunions | Feeling that you are following the wrong direction in life and making choices that limit your growth. | I am moving forward with joy. I am always on the right path. |
| Burns | Burning up inside. Angry with somebody close to you. | I am in harmony with myself and my environment. I balance life easily. |

| Symptom | Emotional Meaning | Affirmations to Heal |
|---|---|---|
| Burping/belching | Feeling limited, burdened, not free. | I am a free spirit. I make my own choices with ease. |
| Bursitis | Stuck in an old pattern. | I forgive and let go easily. |
| Callus formation | Becoming hard on yourself. Stuck. | I release the past and embrace the new every day. |
| Cancer | Carrying deep hurt and longstanding resentment. | I release the past and step into a new life. Only Love flows through my body now. |
| Candida | Feeling frustrated, scattered, demanding and untrusting in your relationship. | I allow myself to be attractive, appealing, and fascinating. I am true to myself. |
| Canker sores | Inability to speak for yourself. Insecure, unsafe, unconfident. | I enjoy being me. I express myself truthfully with Love. |
| Carpal tunnel syndrome | Stop enjoying your work. Feel that life is unfair. | I am creating a beautiful life. Everything goes as it should be. |
| Car sickness | Fear of losing control. | I surrender to the flow of life. I trust life. |
| Cataracts | Seeing too many obstacles in life and dark futures. | I love my life. I anticipate every moment with joy. |
| Cellulite | Feeling unstable, uncertain, and doubtful. | I feel confident to be me. I love my life and life experiences. |

| Symptom | Emotional Meaning | Affirmations to Heal |
|---|---|---|
| Cerebral palsy | Needing love and affection from family. | I bring Love to my family. |
| Cervical cancer | Feeling uncomfortable with your femininity. | I am a powerful and loving woman. I love myself. |
| Chest congestion | Letting people control your life. | I am free and they are free. I am in total harmony with the world. |
| Chicken pox | Feeling irritated, annoyed, unappreciated, used, and unnoticed. | I am loving and loved. |
| Childhood diseases | Feeling upset, left out, unsure how to deal with life. | This child deserves Love. |
| Chills | Uncomfortable about a situation. Internal conflict. | I am in harmony with myself and others. |
| Chlamydia | Feeling rejected, ashamed, used, unvalued. | I love and value myself. My self-love is unconditional. |
| Cholesterol | Feeling insecure, vulnerable, and unprotected. | I am open to receiving Love. Only Love and Joy flow through my system. |
| Chronic fatigue syndrome | Losing your own power | I am a strong and powerful person. My power is always with me. |
| Chronic illness | Not feeling safe in this world. | I am safe, secure, supported and protected. Life loves me. |

## HOW TO HEAL USING INTUITIVE HEALING

| Symptom | Emotional Meaning | Affirmations to Heal |
|---|---|---|
| Circulation problems | Unable to express your emotions in a constructive way. | I express myself with Love and Joy. |
| Claustrophobia | Imprisoned in your own little world. | I am a free spirit. I am safe. |
| Cluster headaches | Feeling attacked and criticised. Thinking too much. | I'm relaxed. I enjoy my life now. I let go of all thoughts. |
| Coeliac disease | Very sensitive, vulnerable and easily irritated. | I am strong and courageous. I enjoy my inner strength. |
| Colds | Overwhelm. Stressed. | I am peaceful and relaxed. I surrender to the present moment. |
| Cold sores | Inability to express your own emotions and needs. | I express myself with Love. Love is my Power. |
| Colic | Feeling irritated, stressed. Too much on your plate. | I am peaceful, calm, and relaxed. I surrender in Love. |
| Colitis | Stuck in the past. | I forgive and release the past now. Every day is a new beginning. |
| Coma | Wanting to escape from life. | I surrender to the present moment. |
| Compulsive eating | Trying to numb painful emotions. | I love and respect myself. I listen to my body. |
| Constipation | Stuck in old way of thinking. | I lovingly release the past and start a new life. Every day is a new beginning. |

| Symptom | Emotional Meaning | Affirmations to Heal |
|---|---|---|
| Convulsions | Internal conflict with your dark side. | I understand my shadow side. I allow Love to replace it. |
| Corns | Being hard on yourself. | I am loving and gentle with myself. |
| Cough | Overwhelmed with stress that comes from other people. | I am loved and appreciated by other people. I love myself. |
| Cramps | Too much stress and struggle. Fear of the future. | I am in peace with myself and others. |
| Crohn's disease | Very negative attitude to life. | I love my life and life experiences. Everything as it should be. |
| Crying | Releasing your emotions. | I rejoice being me. I love and approve of myself. |
| Cushing's syndrome | Overwhelmed by stress. Giving up. | I lovingly balance my thoughts and feelings. My mind and heart are at peace. |
| Cystic fibrosis | Thinking that life is too difficult. | I move nicely with the flow of Life. Life loves me and I love Life. |
| Cyst | Believing that you cannot fulfil your dreams. | I create my life with Love and Joy. I am good enough. |
| Dandruff | Trying to please other people. | I care for myself as much as I care for others. I love me. |

| Symptom | Emotional Meaning | Affirmations to Heal |
|---|---|---|
| Deafness | Not liking what you hear. Saying, "I don't want to hear this." | I trust the process of Life. I am a part of the bigger whole. |
| Dementia | Cannot deal with life anymore. | My life is beautiful at any time. I am safe and secure where I am. |
| Depression | Stuck in victimhood. | I proclaim that, I am the creator of my life. I create loving and empowered experiences. |
| Depression postnatal | Feeling separated, detached, empty, abandon and overwhelmed. | I am a good mother. I enjoy my new experiences. |
| Dermatitis | Uncomfortable in your own skin. | I enjoy being me. |
| Diabetes type 1 | Craving for sweetness and attention. | My life is beautiful and sweet. I love myself and others. |
| Diabetes type 2 | Needy. Self-esteem comes from being helpful to others. Losing identity trying to please others. | I am lovable without being needed. I am worthy. |
| Diarrhea | Regretting your own decisions. | Everything is as it should be. I love my life. |
| Diverticulitis | Losing hope and sabotaging yourself. | I flow easily with life. I am grateful for my life and life experiences. |
| Dizziness | Feeling unbalanced, scattered, stressed. | I am peaceful, relaxed and centred. My life is good. |

| Symptom | Emotional Meaning | Affirmations to Heal |
|---|---|---|
| Down syndrome | A karmic choice to come here to teach parents unconditional love. | This child is pure Love. |
| Drug addictions | Escaping from life difficulties. | I am wonderful the way I am. I choose to connect to my Higher Power. I enjoy being me. |
| Duodenal problems | Stuck in limited ways of thinking. | I forgive myself and forgive others. I let go and start anew. |
| Dysentery | Your body is rebelling. Something needs to change. | I am at peace with myself and others. I listen to my body and I am willing to change. |
| Dyslexia | Wanting to do things in your own way. | I am lovable the way I am. I am happy to be me. |
| Earache | Not wanting to listen to your own inner voice. | I trust my intuition. I listen to my body and accept my truth. |
| Eclampsia | Fear of the future and extra responsibilities. | I welcome new experiences and embrace my new life. |
| Eczema | Bottled up anger, frustration, and self-rejection. | I am in full harmony. I surrender with Love and Peace. Life loves me. |
| Edema | Holding on to unresolved past issues. | I release the past and embrace the new. I forgive myself and others. |

## HOW TO HEAL USING INTUITIVE HEALING

| Symptom | Emotional Meaning | Affirmations to Heal |
|---|---|---|
| Emphysema | Believing that life is a struggle. | I am free and they are free. I love and enjoy my life. |
| Encephalitis (viral) | Listening to the negative mind which leads to more negativity and frustration. | I listen to my intuition. I feel my body. I am calm. |
| Endometriosis | Rejecting your femininity. | I am a strong and beautiful woman. I feel my feminine power. |
| Epilepsy | Feeling attacked and criticised by others. | I am at peace with myself. Harmony surrounds me. |
| Epstein-Barr virus | Disconnected from your own self. | I love and approve of myself. I am good enough and worthy of good things. Life loves me. |
| Fainting | Needing a way out. | I have the power to change my life. I know what I need. |
| Fat | Using fat as a buffer to protect yourself from the energy of others. | I am safe and protected. I release the old patterns and create a new life. |
| Fatigue | Lost interest in life. | I am inspired by life. There is something new and interesting every day. |
| Female problems | Rejecting femininity. | I enjoy being a woman. |
| Fertility | Hidden fears about becoming a parent. | I love being me. I adore my Inner child. I surrender to Love. |

| Symptom | Emotional Meaning | Affirmations to Heal |
|---|---|---|
| Fever | Angry with others. | I am calm, relaxed, and peaceful. I am cool. |
| Fibroid tumours and cysts | Holding on to the past hurts and disappointments. | I release the past. I forgive others. I create my new life now. |
| Fibromyalgia | Losing your power and becoming disempowered. | I empower myself with ease. Strength flows through me. I rejoice. |
| Flatulence | Overwhelmed with emotions. | I am at peace with myself and others. Harmony surrounds me. |
| Flu / cold | Overwhelmed with mass negativity. | I am in my own power. I create my own reality. The energy of others does not affect me. |
| Food allergy/ sensitivity | Very sensitive to what other people think about you. | I am strong and powerful. The energy of others does not affect me. |
| Frigidity | Disconnected from your own sensuality. | I feel with Love. I am safe. |
| Frozen shoulder | Suppressing and numbing your feelings. | It is safe to feel. Love protects me. |
| Fungus infection | Irritated and annoyed with people. | I release the past and forgive. I am in the Now. |
| Gallstones | Solidified anger, resentment, and grief. | I forgive myself and others. Love and joy flow through me. |

| Symptom | Emotional Meaning | Affirmations to Heal |
|---|---|---|
| Gangrene | Not enjoying life anymore. | I am in total harmony with my thoughts and feelings. Only love flows through my system now. |
| Gastritis | Difficulty digesting life. | I love my life. Every experience is a good one. I am safe. |
| Genital herpes | Hating yourself | I love myself. I forgive myself and others. I enjoy my life. |
| Gingivitis | Very irritated with people and situations. | I express myself with Love. I speak my truth. |
| Glandular fever | Lost the connection with your own self. | I love and approve of myself. I am good enough. I am worthy. |
| Gluten intolerance | Problems with digesting childhood issues. | I release the past and forgive. I embrace the new experiences with Love. |
| Goitre | Unable to speak for yourself. | I am safe to speak my truth. I am free and they are free. |
| Gonorrhoea | Carrying a lot of sexual guilt and shame. | I release the past and forgive. I am safe. |
| Gout | Very stressed, stubborn. | I am safe. I am at peace. I flow with life easily. |
| Grey hair | Believing in age, thinking, 'it's downhill from now.' | I am always young in my spirit. |
| Growth | Nursing hurts, wounds, and disappointments. | I forgive myself and others. I am safe. |

| Symptom | Emotional Meaning | Affirmations to Heal |
|---|---|---|
| Guillain-barre syndrome | Losing your power. Wanting to give up or give in. | I am strong and courageous. My power is with me now. |
| Haemophilia | Family fears of pain and struggle. | I am safe, secure, supported and protected. I am Divinely guided. |
| Haemorrhoids | Holding on to outdated family believes and attitudes. | I release the old and embrace the new. Life is easy for me. |
| Hair loss | Too much pushing and straining. Stop loving and enjoying yourself. | I am peaceful, calm, and loving. I love my life. |
| Hay fever | Bottled up feelings. | I am one with nature. I flow with the natural rhythms. |
| Headaches | You have become too stressed, too serious, judgemental, critical, tired. | I am at peace with myself. I see my life with love. |
| Heart attack | Blocking love and intimacy. | Love and joy are my priority. I bring Love in every experience. |
| Heart blockage | Blocking love and intimacy. | I create Love. All my experiences are beautiful. |
| Heart burn | Difficulty digesting life. | I love all my experiences. I flow with life easily. |
| Hepatitis | Bottled up anger. Stubborn and self-righteous. | I am happy with who I am. I love myself and I love others. |

| Symptom | Emotional Meaning | Affirmations to Heal |
|---|---|---|
| Hernia | Burdened by disappointments in relationships. | I create my life and relationships with love. Love rules my life. |
| Herniated disc | Too much strain and struggle in life. | It is safe to be me. I enjoy my life and life experiences. |
| Hiccups (recurring) | Not speaking your truth. | I speak my truth with ease. I am free to be me. |
| Hip problems | Carrying too many burdens on your hips. | I go with the flow. I always move in the right directions. |
| Hives | Very irritated and annoyed. | I am peaceful and calm. All is well in my life. |
| Hodgkin's disease | Stressed with too many commitments and responsibilities. | I love myself. I am happy with my life. I am at peace with everything. |
| Huntington's disease | Extreme disconnectedness from the self. | I surrender the outcome to the Divine. I am in harmony with myself and with the world. |
| Hyperactivity | Scattered, impulsive, bored, in constant need of change and stimulation. | I am safe, secure, supported and protected. I am at peace. Life loves me. |
| Hypertension | Pushing hard to achieve. | I gently flow with life. Life co-operates with me. Everything as it should be. |

| Symptom | Emotional Meaning | Affirmations to Heal |
|---|---|---|
| Hyperthyroidism (overactive thyroids) | Rushing too much and not expressing your needs and emotions. | I express myself with love. Harmony surrounds me. I am calm. |
| Hyperventilation | Holding on to worry, stress, and negative thoughts. Feeling out of control. | I am calm and safe. Love flows gently through me. |
| Hypothyroidism (underactive thyroids) | Lack of desire. Loss of interest in life and feeling humiliated. | I release the old and allow new things to come. I love my life. I love myself. |
| Hypotension (low blood pressure) | Giving up your power to others. | I am powerful, strong, and courageous. My strength is always with me. |
| Immune system (weak) | Too much insecurity and inner conflict. | I am safe, secure, supported and protected. I love life. |
| Impotence | Feeling betrayed, angry, and rejected. | I love myself. I allow my sexuality to thrive through all expressions of life. I am sensual. |
| Incontinence | Feeling out of control. | I allow myself to feel. I listen to my body. I learn from my emotions. |
| Indigestion | Difficulty digesting new experiences. | I love my life. I digest all my experiences with love and ease. |
| Infection | Feeling invaded and attacked. Giving up. | I chose peace, harmony, and love. I am safe. |

## HOW TO HEAL USING INTUITIVE HEALING

| Symptom | Emotional Meaning | Affirmations to Heal |
|---|---|---|
| Infertility | Thinking that there is too much struggle to be a woman. | I love being a woman. I create life with ease, love, and joy. |
| Inflammation | Suppressed anger. | I am calm, peaceful, and serene. All is well in me and around me. |
| Insanity | Trying to escape and withdraw from life. | I am a part of the Divine. Life takes me where I need to be. I trust the Divine flow. I am at peace. |
| Insomnia | Too much tension, guilt, fear. | My body is relaxed, and my mind is peaceful. I am falling asleep right now. |
| Irritable bowel syndrome | Focusing on a negative side of life. | I love myself. I love my live. I am doing the best. |
| Itching | Too many unexpressed emotions. | I am happy where I am. I am peaceful, relaxed and content. |
| Jaundice | Stressed, irritated, confused, angry and uptight. | I love my life and all the people around me. I am content with what I have. I am at peace. |
| Jaw problems | Having problems with many facets of communication. | I speak my truth effortlessly. I express myself with ease. |
| Joint problems | Feeling overwhelmed by the responsibilities of caring for family and friends. | I take care of myself as much as I take care for others. I love me. |

| Symptom | Emotional Meaning | Affirmations to Heal |
|---|---|---|
| Keratitis | Confused, angry, irritated. Unclear life directions. | I see with Love. I belong where I am. I am moving in the right direction. |
| Kidney failure | Losing your power due to low self-esteem and blame. | Each experience is the opportunity for growth. I grow stronger every day. |
| Kidney stones | Too much fear, hardness, negativity, and inferiority. | I release the past and forgive. Every day is a new beginning. |
| Kleptomania | Suppressed anger. Not belonging. | I belong to the whole of life. Life supports me. I co-operate with life. |
| Lactose intolerance | Insecurity. Believing that life is difficult. | I flow with the process of life. Life loves me. |
| Laryngitis | Laryngitis. Inability to express what you want. | I speak my truth effortlessly. I express myself with Love. |
| Leprosy | Rejection of self. Feeling dirty, rejected, outcast. | I am a pure Divine expression. I am love. I am love. I am love. |
| Leukemia | Seeing life as hard, joyless and a struggle. Family problems. | I forgive myself and others. I move beyond past fears and proclaim myself free. |
| Lips (cracked) | Insecure and not confident. | I am strong and courageous. I express my beauty with ease. |
| Lockjaw | Too much resistance. | I trust life. I express my needs effortlessly. Life co-operates with me. |

| Symptom | Emotional Meaning | Affirmations to Heal |
|---|---|---|
| Lung cancer | Constantly pushing, resisting, and not giving yourself any credit. | My life is in perfect balance. I give and receive equally. Harmony surrounds me. |
| Lupus | Insecurity, lack of confidence and low self-worth. | I am safe, secure, supported and protected. Life loves me. I love life. |
| Lymphoma | Feeling insecure, unsafe, unsupported. | I support myself with Love and Joy. I love myself unconditionally. |
| Lymph problems | Easily influenced and used by others. Confused and lost. | I flow through life with ease. Love surrounds me. |
| Malaria | Feeling unsafe, insecure, and out of balance with life and nature. | I am balanced with life and nature. I flow in the rhythm of Love. |
| Mastitis | Feeling unsupported and abandoned. Trapped and bound by responsibilities. | I am a good mother. I embrace my new role with Love and effortlessness. Life supports me. |
| Measles | Craving for love and attention | I am safe and secure. I love myself. |
| Melanoma | Very dissatisfied with life, thinking, "What's the use?" | I am loved and supported by life itself. Only good comes from every experience. |

| Symptom | Emotional Meaning | Affirmations to Heal |
|---|---|---|
| Memory loss | Having too much fear to remember. Wanting to escape. | I remember Love. Only Love operates within my psyche. |
| Meningitis | Feeling attacked, invaded, threatened. Out of balance. | I am in peace and total balance. I use my mind with Love. Only Love flows through it. |
| Menopausal problems | Problems with expressing your femininity and fear of aging. | I am loving, beautiful and gorgeous at any time. I do not think about biological age. I am pure Love. |
| Menstrual problems | Difficulty being a woman. | I love being a woman. Love governs my body. |
| Metabolic disorders | Difficulty expressing yourself and communicating your own needs and wants. | I love and respect myself. I express my needs with love and freedom. I am free. |
| Migraine | Overcommitting yourself. | I am calm, peaceful, and serene. I flow with life effortlessly. Life co-operates with me. |
| Miscarriage | Fear of childbirth. Unresolved family problems. | I release the past and forgive. I create new every day. Love helps me. |
| Motion sickness | Fear of losing control. | I surrender to the present moment with ease. I trust life. |

| Symptom | Emotional Meaning | Affirmations to Heal |
|---|---|---|
| Mouth ulcers | Inability to express yourself and speaking your truth. | I speak my truth with ease. I express myself with Love. |
| Multiple sclerosis. | Stubborn and inflexible. Driven by fear. | I trust life. I surrender to the present moment. I live only in the Now. |
| Mumps | Inability to express your feelings, wants and desires. | I express myself with ease. I speak my truth. |
| Muscular dystrophy | Hopelessness and helplessness. | I am safe, secure, supported and protected. Life co-operates with me. |
| Nail biting | Anxious about your relationships with others. | I can handle anything life throws at me. I am growing with every experience. |
| Narcolepsy | Trying to escape from life. | Divine helps me, guides me, and protects me. I trust the Divine wisdom within me. |
| Nausea | Feeling trapped in a situation you don't like. | I trust life. Only good can come from any experience. |
| Nervous breakdown | Can't handle life. Have been pushed to the limit. | I embrace my life with Love. I communicate lovingly and truthfully. All is well in my life right now. |

| Symptom | Emotional Meaning | Affirmations to Heal |
|---|---|---|
| Nervousness | Fear of failure, judgement, and rejection. | I see my life with Love. I communicate with ease and joy. |
| Nightmares | Suppressed negative feelings. | I am always safe. I release everything other than Love. Only Love operates in my life. |
| Nodules | Solidified stress, fears. | I release the stress and allow Love to come in. Love flows through me. |
| Nose (bleeding) | Reacting to other people's opinion about you. | I acknowledge my own self-worth. I follow my intuitive guidance. |
| Nose (blocked) | Blocking your intuition. | I follow my intuition. I can smell the air. |
| Nose (runny) | Pushing yourself too hard. | I am gentle with myself. |
| Numbness | Suppressing your feelings. Not wanting to feel. | I allow myself to feel. It is safe to feel. |
| Obesity | Too much insecurity. | I am secure and protected. Life loves me. |
| Obsessive-compulsive disorder | Fear. Trying to control the uncontrollable. | I relax with the flow of life. I trust life. |
| Osteomyelitis | Carrying a deep hurt inside about a major issue in life. | I trust life. I am always safe. Only good comes from all my experiences. |
| Osteoporosis | Inability to express your needs and wants. Losing your power. | I am strong at any time. My strength is always with me. Life supports me. |

## HOW TO HEAL USING INTUITIVE HEALING

| Symptom | Emotional Meaning | Affirmations to Heal |
|---|---|---|
| Ovarian cancer | Holding on to deep disappointments from the past. Feeling betrayed. | I release the past and forgive. Every day is a new beginning. |
| Ovarian cyst | Holding on to old wounds, especially from men. | I create my life with Love. I trust life. |
| Overweight | Feeling stuck. | I flow with the rhythm of Love. I love myself. |
| Panic attack | Feeling attacked, wronged, betrayed. | I am strong, powerful, and courageous. I can handle anything that life throws at me. |
| Paralysis | Can't handle life. Holding on to a trauma. | Life co-operates with me. I flow with the rhythm of Love. I am strong in my own way. |
| Paranoia | Out of control. Constantly anticipating something bad to happen. | I am in total peace and harmony. I surrender to the Divine. |
| Parasites | Giving away your life force to others. Feeling that people feed off you. | I claim my power back. I am strong and independent. |
| Parathyroid problems | Disappointed with life. Inability to communicate your own needs. | I release the past and forgive. I express myself easily. I speak my truth. |
| Parkinson's disease | Too much fear and resistance. Trying to control everything and everyone. | I trust and surrender to the Divine flow of life. I am always safe and secure. |

| Symptom | Emotional Meaning | Affirmations to Heal |
| --- | --- | --- |
| Peptic ulcer | Too much stress, worry, anxiety and uncertainty | I embrace my life with love and ease. I love myself. I am at peace. |
| Pimples | Uncomfortable in your own skin. | I love and respect myself. I am beautiful. |
| Pneumonia | Disappointed with life. Thinking, "What is the point? It's all too hard ..." | I balance my emotions easily. Only good comes from all my experiences. Life loves me. |
| Post-traumatic stress disorder | Holding on to the past. Stuck and unable to move on. | I surrender myself to the present moment. I live in the now. |
| Premature birth | Stress, impatience, discomfort. Baby doesn't want to stay in an uncomfortable or hostile environment. | I surrender to the natural flow of life. I am one with nature. I am peaceful and serene. |
| Premenstrual syndrome | Having problems with being a woman. | I love being a woman. |
| Prostate cancer | Fear of aging and losing your masculinity. | I love my masculinity. I am always young in my spirit. |
| Psoriasis | Uncomfortable in your own skin. | I am safe, secure, supported and protected. I love myself. |
| Rash | Insecurity and high sensitivity. | I am calm, relaxed, and serene. I am comfortable in my body. |
| Repetitive strain injury | Not listening to your body. Pushing yourself hard. | I listen to my body. I follow my intuition. I love myself. |

## HOW TO HEAL USING INTUITIVE HEALING

| Symptom | Emotional Meaning | Affirmations to Heal |
|---|---|---|
| Restless leg syndrome | Resisting to do something until you can't stand it and your legs want to move forward. | I surrender myself to the Divine flow. I live in the now. I am centred. |
| Rheumatism | Inflexible, stubborn, domineering. Trying to be right rather than loving. Difficulty forgiving. | I release the past and forgive easily. I flow with the rhythm of Love. I live in the now. |
| Rheumatoid arthritis | Inflexible, serious, critical, and judgmental. Too much righteousness and perfectionism. | I am flexible and gentle with myself. I love my life. |
| Rickets | Starving for warmth, support, love, and nourishment. | Love flows through me. I allow Love to take over and rule my life. |
| Ring worms | Somebody is getting under your skin. Irritated with people. | I am a loving operator of my life. I am free. |
| Root canal | Rejecting a part of yourself. | I embrace all parts of myself. I express myself freely and with love. I love my life. |
| Rosacea | Carrying guilt, embarrassment, and shame. | I love and approve myself. I am a beautiful person. I have the power to heal. |
| Scabies | Becoming impatient and irritable. Infected thinking. | I am a loving operator of my life. I am free. |
| Scarring | Past wounds. Unresolved emotions. | I release the past and forgive. I trust life. |

| Symptom | Emotional Meaning | Affirmations to Heal |
|---|---|---|
| Sciatica | Living in the past. Having unresolved childhood issues. | I move with ease and grace. I live in the now. I trust life. |
| Scleroderma | Self-loathing. Not wanting to participate in life. | I love my life. I trust life. Life always supports me. |
| Scoliosis | Feeling insecure and unsupported. | I am safe, secure, supported and protected. Life supports me. |
| Seizure | Suppressed trauma. Inability to express your feelings. | I am a part of the Divine. The Universe always supports me. I am safe. |
| Senility | Returning to a childlike state to escape from life and responsibilities. | I am peaceful. I am calm. I am one with Love. I still trust life. |
| Shingles | Unworthiness and low self-esteem that come from childhood. | I love myself and my life. I forgive and release the past. I am worthy of good things. |
| Sinusitis | Irritation with people and wanting to keep them at a distance. Family issues. | I am in total harmony with everybody and myself. |
| Skin dry | Loss of inspiration and vitality. Feeling disconnected from your purpose. | I love my life. I participate in every life experience with joy. |
| Skin oily | Trying to please others in order to be liked. | I am loved and likable. I love myself. I am important. |

## HOW TO HEAL USING INTUITIVE HEALING

| Symptom | Emotional Meaning | Affirmations to Heal |
|---|---|---|
| Sleep apnoea | Not trusting life. Unexpressed anger and disappointments. | I trust life. Every moment is filled with joy and love. |
| Sleep problems | Thinking too much. | My body is relaxed, and my mind is peaceful. I am falling asleep right now. |
| Slipped disk | Difficulty making decisions on major issues. | I support myself with Love. I follow through my decisions with ease. |
| Smell (loss of) | Loss of intuition. | I listen to my body. I follow my intuition. |
| Snoring | Stubborn. Stuck in an old way of thinking and doing. | I release the past and embrace the new. Only the energy of Love operates within me now. |
| Social anxiety | Fear of being judged and criticised. | I am safe, secure, supported and protected. Life co-operates with me. |
| Sore throat | Not speaking your truth. | I speak my truth. I express myself with Love. |
| Spasm | Holding on to stressful thoughts. | I am calm, peaceful, and serene. I forgive and let go easily. |
| Spastic colitis | Cannot let go of stressful issues in life. Focused on problems rather than on solutions. | I am safe to live my life the way I want. Life always co-operates with me. I trust life. |

| Symptom | Emotional Meaning | Affirmations to Heal |
|---|---|---|
| Sprain | Stressed and overworked. Too many responsibilities. | I trust that everything happens for my higher good. I am safe. I am calm. |
| Stiffness | Feeling stuck and limited. Having, 'My way or no way' mentality. | I am flexible. I am gentle with myself. I flow easily with life. |
| Stomach ulcer | Continuously on hyper drive. Driven to produce. Competitive. | Life co-operates with me. I digest new experiences with ease. I am calm and relaxed. |
| Stretch marks | Feeling uncomfortable in your own skin. Judging and criticising yourself and your body. | I am comfortable with myself. I love my body. I love my life. |
| Stuttering | Not being able to express what you really feel. Suppressing your emotions. | I can speak up for myself easily. I express myself with Love. I am safe. |
| Sunstroke | Not being careful and not taking enough care of yourself. Having rebellious attitudes. | I take care for myself. I listen to my body. I follow my intuition. |
| Swelling (Edema, Fluid retention) | Too much thinking, not enough feeling and sensing. Being stuck in negative beliefs about your life, health, and success. | I allow myself to feel. I release all thoughts and I bring myself to the present moment. I feel Love. |

## HOW TO HEAL USING INTUITIVE HEALING

| Symptom | Emotional Meaning | Affirmations to Heal |
|---|---|---|
| Syphilis | Giving away your power to others. | I am a strong person. I can protect myself. My power is within me. |
| Tapeworm | Feeling like a victim, helpless and hopeless. | I am a powerful person. My strength is within me. I am free and independent. |
| Teeth grinding | Stressed and overwhelmed with everyday issues. | I release all tension. I fill myself with Love. I am peaceful and serene. |
| Tooth decay | Inability to express yourself. Difficulty making major life decisions. | I am a decisive person. I know what I want. I make the right choices. |
| Thrombosis | Sabotaging yourself. Stuck in an old way of thinking. | I release the past and forgive. I allow joy to run throw my system. Joy surrounds me. |
| Thrush | Trying to control your relationships or letting others control you. | I allow myself to be attractive, appealing, and fascinating. I am true to myself. |
| Tics/Twitches | Feeling fearful and apprehensive about yourself. | I am safe to be me. Only my own approval of myself matters. I love myself. |
| Tinnitus | Do not want to listen anymore. Not hearing your inner voice. In great need of relaxation. | I trust the process of life. I listen to my body. I follow my intuition. I can relax and rest. |

| Symptom | Emotional Meaning | Affirmations to Heal |
|---|---|---|
| Tonsillitis | Suppressing your emotions, creativity, and joy. | I express myself with love and joy. Communication is easy for me. |
| Tourette's syndrome | Feeling stressed, frustrated, confused and out of control. Not trusting yourself and your body. | I feel safe to be me. I trust myself. I trust life. All experiences are good experiences. |
| Tuberculosis | Too much inner turmoil and struggle. | Life always supports me. I trust life. I love life. I am safe. |
| Tumours | Holding on to old wounds, hurts and trauma. Cannot forgive and let go. | I release the past and step into a new life. Only Love flows through my body now. |
| Ulcer | There is something that is eating you away. What could this be? | I love myself. I accept myself. Only good comes from all my experiences. |
| Underweight | Denying nourishment, loving attention, and care. | I support myself with love. I allow myself to take nourishment in. I am safe. |
| Urinary tract infection | Pissed off with the opposite sex or partner. | I am at peace with myself. I release the old and welcome a new life. |
| Vaginitis | Carrying sexual guilt. | I am a beautiful and sexual being. Other people's energies do not affect me. I am safe. |

| Symptom | Emotional Meaning | Affirmations to Heal |
|---|---|---|
| Varicose veins | Inability to move forward. Feeling that you are being trapped in a situation you hate. | I move with ease and joy. I love life. Life loves me back. I am free. |
| Venereal disease | Too much sexual guilt, shame, and humiliation. | I love and accept myself. I am worthy of love. I am good. |
| Vertigo | Feeling scattered, unsafe, unstable, and out of control. Cannot cope with life anymore. | I am centred, calm and peaceful. Life supports me. I am safe. |
| Vomiting | Your body is rejecting the stress, wrong ideas, heaviness, and feelings of being trapped. | I am balanced. Harmony surrounds me. What I think and what I feel are the same. I listen to my intuition. |
| Warts | Focusing on things you hate. | I focus on Love. |
| Water retention | Holding on to negative beliefs about your life, health, and success. | I gently flow with the process of life. I release the old and embrace the new. |
| Whiplash | This is a sign that in some areas of life you need to change. | I listen to my body with Love. I follow my intuition. |
| Worms (parasites) | Allowing other people to feed off you. | I am strong and independent. I surround myself with Love. |

# Afterword

Writing this book has been a journey towards discovering my own Intuitive Healing Power. I have realised that intuitive development is a lifelong process, and we should never stop developing our intuition.

> "You must train your intuition – you must trust the small voice inside you which tells you exactly what to say, what to decide." – Ingrid Bergman

I am incredibly grateful for the opportunity to do what I do. Every day I start my morning with expressing the words of gratitude to those who are with me and who give me strength, courage, inspiration, and love. I often say, "Thank you, Universe, for all the things in my life that I know and don't know about yet. I am so grateful for my life."

I love my life and my work. When I look back at my life, I can see how much I have grown because of my intuition.

During the years of medical training, I cultivated a great respect for the rational mind - the logic part that takes no more than 10% of our mind capacity. Now I am on a journey of exploring the intuitive mind which takes at least 90% of our consciousness. I believe this is a lifelong pursuit. You cannot achieve a quick enlightenment or suddenly arrive. You must go through a journey that includes problems, pains, aches, and illnesses. The most demanding intuitive challenge is to search for the light in any situation, even when things seem to be totally unfair. A hard lesson, certainly. But one well learned.

I noticed that sometimes problems cannot be stopped no matter what we do. But the more peaceful we become, the better chance we have to cultivate peace inside and around us. It can only be achieved with energy awareness and regular meditation.

Intuitive healing made me realise that all people, does not matter where they are in the world, desire the same things – good health, happiness, joy, connection, peace of mind, love, abundance, and freedom. The spiritual truth of the tribal chakra: 'All is One,' can heal, transform, and nourish the whole planet and the collective human soul.

I genuinely believe that this is the way we are going now. The age of Aquarius has started in 2020 and the Coronavirus pandemic is the transition mechanism to help us move from the physical era into the energy era.

Good Luck to all of us on this wonderful journey!

I would love to hear your feedback and your stories about your healing and transformation using your Intuitive Healing Power. Please contact me through my website
http://dririnawebster.com/

> *"The more you trust your intuition, the more empowered you become, the stronger you become, and the happier you become."*
>
> — Gisele Bundchen

# Final Note:

I hope that this book brings you greater understanding and knowledge of what is unseen but essential – the energy. May you be filled with positive energy of love, purpose, and trust.

I wish you happiness, peace, joy, and success. Know that you are greatly loved by the Universe that supports you on your journey. Everything is working out for your highest good. All is well.

Love to you.
Irina

# About the Author

Dr Irina Webster is a medical doctor, who, following her retirement from the conventional medical industry, promotes the value of Medical Intuition and Intuitive Healing to the world. She is the founder of, 'Intuitive Healing Power' – an organisation that provides Intuitive Healing and Medical Intuition practitioner training programs. She is an author of many best-selling books about intuitive health and wellness.

Passionate about what makes people healthy and what makes them sick, Irina is on a mission to join science and spirituality in a way that not only facilitates the health of the individual but also heals humanity.

Since her early interest in Psychoneuroimmunology in the 90th in Russia, she became aware of how negative emotions predispose us not only to stress but to disease, she began investigating ways on how to pinpoint the exact emotions that contribute to illness and then release them from the body, opening us up to greater love and compassion for ourselves and others.

Irina conducts Medical Intuition and Intuitive Healing workshops and courses, both online and off-line. She conducts private and public Intuitive Healing sessions, and Intuitive Healing meditations in Australia and all over the world. Her website http://dririnawebster.com is where you can find and participate in different intuitive healing programs and courses.

# Bibliography

Schmale, A.H., "Giving up as a Final Common Pathway to Changes in Health," Advances in Psychosomatic Medicine 8 (1972)

Sarason, I.G., et al., "Life Events, Social Support, and Illness," Psychosomatic Medicine 47, no. 2 (March- April 1985)

Thomas, C.B., and K.R. Duszynski, "Closeness to Parents and Family Constellation in a Prospective Study of Five Disease States," The Johns Hopkins Medical Journal 134 (1974)

Mason, J.M., "Psychological Stress and Endocrine Function," in E.J. Sachar, ed., Topics in Psychoendocrinology (New York: Grune & Stratton, 1975)

Reiter, R.C., "Occult Somatic Pathology in Women with Chronic Pelvic Pain," Clinical Obstetrics and Gynecology 33, no. 1 (March 1990)

Slade, P., "Sexual Attitudes and Social Role Orientations in Infertile Women," Journal of Psychosomatic Research 25, no. 3 (1981)

Weil, R.J., and C. Tupper, "Personality, Life Situation, and Communication: A Study of Habitual Abortion," Psychosomatic Medicine 22, no. 6 (November 1960)

Alvarez, W.C., Nervousness, Indigestion, and Pain (New York: Hoeber, 1943).

Dunbar, F., Emotions and Bodily Changes, 3d ed. (New York: Columbia University Press, 1947).

Alexander, F., Psychosomatic Medicine (London: George Allen & Unwin, Ltd., 1952)

Bacon, C.L., et al., "A Psychosomatic Survey of Cancer of the Breast," Psychosomatic Medicine 14, no. 6 (November 1952)

Kalis, B.L., et al., "Personality and Life History Factors in Persons Who Are Potentially Hypertensive," The Journal of Nervous and Mental Disease 132 (June 1961)

Krantz, D.S., and D.C. Glass, "Personality, Behavior Patterns, and Physical Illness," in W.D. Gentry, ed., Handbook of Behavioral Medicine (New York: Guilford, 1984).

Booth, G., "Psychodynamics in Parkinsonism," Psychosomatic Medicine 10, no. 1 (January 1948)

Cloninger, C.R., "Brain Networks Underlying Personality Development," in B.J. Carroll and J.E. Barrett, eds., Psychopathology and the Brain (New York: Raven Press, 1991)

Groen, J.J., "Psychosomatic Aspects of Ménière's Disease," Acta Oto-laryngologica 95, no. 5–6 (May–June 1983)

Mitscherlich, M., "The Psychic State of Patients Suffering from Parkinsonism," Advances in Psychosomatic Medicine 1 (1960)

Adams, D.K., et al., "Early Clinical Manifestations of Disseminated Sclerosis," British Medical Journal 2, no. 4676 (August 19, 1950)

## Books:

Master Choa Kok Sui. *Advanced Pranic Healing*. IIS Publishing Foundation, Inc. 2012.

Stephen Co (Author), Eric B. Robins (Author). *Your Hands Can Heal You: Pranic Healing Energy Remedies to Boost Vitality and Speed Recovery from Common Health Problems*. Atria Books, 2007.

Judith Orloff. *Emotional Freedom: Liberate Yourself from Negative Emotions and Transform Your Life*. CROWN, 2011.

Louise L. Hay, Mona Lisa Schulz. *All Is Well: Heal Your Body with Medicine, Affirmations and Intuition*. Hay House, 2013

Caroline Myss. *Anatomy of the Spirit: The Seven Stages of Power and Healing*. Harmony, 1997.

Caroline Myss. *Sacred Contracts: Awakening Your Divine Potential*. BANTAM AUSTRALIA LICENSE , 2002.

Sonia Choquette. *The Psychic Pathway*. CROWN,1995.

Gary Zukav. *The Seat of the Soul*. Simon & Schuster, 2014

Judith Orloff. *Positive Energy: 10 Extraordinary Prescriptions for Transforming Fatigue, Stress, and Fear Into Vibrance, Strength, and Love*. CROWN, 2005.

Judith Orloff. *Second Sight: An Intuitive Psychiatrist Tells Her Extraordinary Story and Shows You How to Tap Your Own Inner Wisdom*. Random House, 2010

# Also Available from Dr Irina Webster

## "The Secret Energy of Your Body. Intuitive Healing Guide." Book

By Dr Irina Webster

Energy is the root of body and mind. When energy flows through the body properly, you are in a state of health.

When there is an energetic disturbance in the body, a disease state is created.

Illnesses manifest in the body's energy, 'energy body' before it manifests in the physical body. Healing occurs in the energy field before it becomes apparent in the physical body.

The root causes of the energetic disturbances that create illnesses are trapped thoughts and emotions stored in the cells of the body. These trapped

thoughts and emotions are not necessary yours but can originate from your family and ancestors.

'The Secret Energy of Your Body,' reveals how to:

- Heal yourself from within: Your emotions, your energy, and your thoughts.
- Learn how to love your illness instead of hating it because it is the message from your body about your life.
- Learn how your body talks to you, and how you should communicate with it.
- Pinpoint specific emotional patterns that lead to disease and create problems.
- Connect to the energetic frequencies of colour and use them to heal your emotions.
- Understand the emotional/energetic messages from your body and its lessons.

In 'The Secret Energy of Your Body,' Dr Irina Webster provides an in-depth, practical resource for anyone who desires a safe, easy and effective way to heal yourself and help others.

Available from http://dririnawebster.com

## 'Chromotherapy Healing' cards.

By Dr Irina Webster
47 cards and a guidebook

'Chromotherapy Healing' cards are your unique tool to unlocking the extraordinary healing power of colour. Colour healing can be used very effectively to treat many problems: Physical, emotional, and spiritual.

Dr Irina Webster has researched how to balance 5 senses (visual, hearing, smell, taste, touch) in order to heal your body and soul. The cards will show you:

- What colour to wear each day to help yourself heal
- What gemstone to carry with you to evoke the energy of each colour
- What music to listen to in order to sense each colour
- What smell can help you connect to a particular colour
- What food to eat to feel the energy of each colour
- What plants to grow in your garden to enhance the power of each colour.

Available from www.dririnawebster.com

# Intuitive Healing CDs and guided Meditations.

1. **'Overcome Stress Naturally with Intuitive Healing.'**
Guided Meditation (1-hour)
This CD will help you to overcome stress naturally using your own intuitive healing power. Step by step you will be guided to heal yourself.

2. **'Release Your Pain with Intuitive Healing.'**
Guided Meditation (1- hour)
This CD will assist you to activate your own intuitive healing ability and help to relieve pain naturally. You will be guided to clean out the blockages and the densities from the place that is in pain. You will also be guided to heal negative emotions and create more joy, happiness, and pleasure in your life.

### 3. 'Body Scan Meditation with Intuitive Healing.'
Guided Meditation (1-hour)

The purpose of body scan meditation is to study the entire body, part by part. It is like going through your whole body with an x-ray machine checking organ by organ, muscle by muscle and bone by bone.

### 4. 'Progressive Muscle Relaxation with Intuitive Healing.'
Guided Meditation (1-hour)

Progressive relaxation helps you control the state of tension in your muscles. Step by step you'll be guided to relax and experience a joyful and loving state.

Available from www.dririnawebster.com

## 'Healthy Pregnancy from A to Z: An Expectant Parent's Guide to Wellness.' Book

By Dr Irina Webster
Intuitive Pregnancy Book.

Pregnancy is a highly intuitive time in a woman's life. Your intuition or 'six sense' naturally increases and you can use this to stay healthy and vibrant. More importantly, you can connect to your baby and keep this sacred bond from the time of conception and even earlier.

    Pregnancy and Intuition.
    Mother and Baby Intuitive Bond.
    Father and Baby Intuitive Bond.

Questions arise such as what is healthy to eat? Should I exercise and how? What lifestyle should I have? What to believe in while pregnant? What about relaxation and maintaining good relationships? Are pre-pregnancy preparations important?

This book is a deep exploration of the most important question, 'How to Be Healthy during Pregnancy?' And it shows you a way to health and wellbeing while expecting a child.

By reading this book, you will discover:

- Five Healthy Pregnancy Principles.
- The healthiest things to do each month during pregnancy.

- Your baby's development, what they can do and what they can sense each week throughout the duration of the pregnancy.
- Twenty-one Best pregnancy foods.
- How to maintain your sex life during pregnancy.
- Seven healing meditation techniques for pregnancy.
- Special exercise complexes during pregnancy.
- Beneficial yoga poses for different stages of pregnancy.
- Thirteen ways to bond with your unborn child.
- The safe herbal remedies to heal pregnancy complaints.
- Natural ways to keep your skin, hair, and teeth beautiful during pregnancy.
- How to love your pregnant body.
- Several techniques on self-massage to heal and rejuvenate you during pregnancy.
- How a father-to-be can be a loving partner and a caring dad.
- How to quit your bad habits during pregnancy.
- How music can benefit your pregnancy and what kind of music you should avoid when expecting.
- Steps to ensure a healthy birth and fast, natural recovery.

# On-line Courses and Professional Trainings:

## 5 WEEKS TO FORGIVENESS: HOW TO FORGIVE COURSE

In this course you will learn:
- Essential steps in How to Forgive.
- How to Forgive yourself.
- Forgiveness using Past life experiences.
- Energy Anatomy of Forgiveness.
- Fill your heart with Loving-kindness.

Available from www.dririnawebster.com

## HOW TO MAKE AN INTUITIVE DIAGNOSIS

- How to make an intuitive diagnosis on yourself and on other people.
- How to make an intuitive diagnosis before you see a client and then, when you are with a client.
- How to read the body signs and interpret them.
- How to read people's names.
- How to scan the body energetically.
- How to ask your intuition for help and guidance.
- How to interpret your intuitive impression.

Available from www.dririnawebster.com

# HOW TO SCAN YOUR OWN BODY WITH ENERGY MEDICINE

In this course you will learn how to:

- Scan Your Own Body layer by layer like a x-ray vison.
- Identify the energetic blockages in the body and release them.
- Activate your, 'inner eye' – the natural ability to see your body from the inside.
- Sense the, 'subtle body energy' inside the organs.
- Scan the body of other people (after learning how to scan your own body).

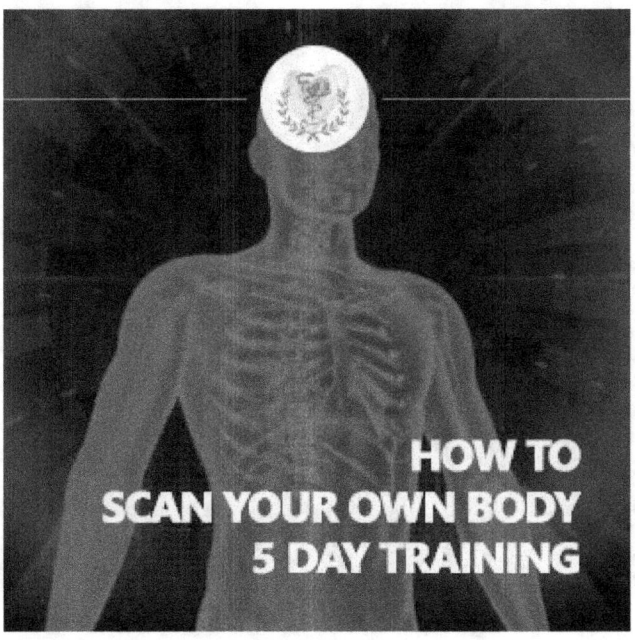

Available from www.dririnawebster.com

## HOW TO TALK TO YOUR BODY AND ORGANS

In this course you will:

- Learn to connect to your own organs.
- Learn to understand your body's (organs) messages.
- Learn to sense the subtle body energy.
- Learn to communicate with your own body.
- Learn what different body shapes tell us.

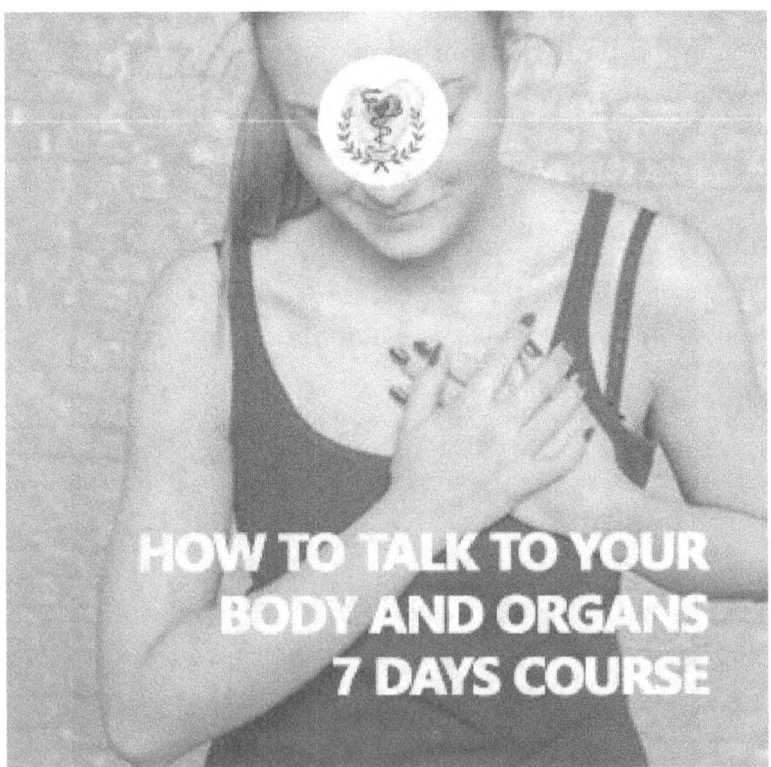

Available from www.dririnawebster.com

DR IRINA WEBSTER

## HOW TO REMOVE EMOTIONS FROM THE BODY

In this course you will learn:

- How to identify where in the body the emotions are trapped.
- How to remove the trapped emotions from the body/organs.
- How to balance the organ(s) after releasing the trapped emotions.

Available from www.dririnawebster.com

## BECOMING AN INTUITIVE HEALER AND A MEDICAL INTUITIVE

In this course you will learn how to:

- Connect to organs and sense energy in the organs.
- Body scan on yourself and others.
- How to make an intuitive diagnosis.
- How to read the body.
- How your hands can heal you.
- Human Energetic Anatomy and how to use it for diagnosis and healing.
- Reading intuitive information from people's names.
- Working with Healing dreams, hypnagogic states, and lucid dreaming.
- How to ask your intuition for help and guidance.
- How to interpret your intuitive impressions.

Available from www.dririnawebster.com

# "CURE YOUR EATING DISORDER: 5 Step Program to Change Your Brain. Neuroplasticity Approach." Book

**By Dr Irina Webster**

What are the 5 Neuroplasticity Steps that will stop any Eating Disorder (even the most long-standing ones)?

1. Believe that you can stop your bulimia disorders
   Do exercises to begin changing the way your mind works.
2. Re- Identify
   Recognise the false nature of your bulimia disorder thoughts.
3. Re-Symbolise
   Escape from loop thinking that feeds the bulimia disorder.
4. Re-Direct
   Defeat recurrent thoughts that give power to the bulimia disorder.
5. Re-Evaluate
   De-value and ignore harmful urges until they start to fade away.

Once you learn and practice these five steps, your eating disorder will start to fade away.

## HOW TO HEAL USING INTUITIVE HEALING

**The book will make you able to:**

- Make permanent positive changes to the structure and function of your brain associated with stopping eating disorder behaviours.
- Stop the little voices in the head that tell you to starve or binge and purge.
- Change your feelings and sensations to the best so that you don't have to use an eating disorder to make up for them.
- Stop the, 'broken eye syndrome' – when you see a fat person in a mirror when you are actually very slim.
- Have control over your anorexic or bulimic thoughts and be able to tune them out of your brain.
- Restore your feelings of hunger and of fullness sensations.
- Restore your self-esteem, feelings of control and decision-making abilities.

Available from http://www.eating-disorders-books.com/

www.ingramcontent.com/pod-product-compliance
Lightning Source LLC
Chambersburg PA
CBHW071350290426
44108CB00014B/1488